Before  *in*

The Histo

by
Richard Ginn, Ronald Reeve
&
Andrew Campbell

MMXIII

© Copyright Richard J. Ginn 2013
© Copyright Ronald Reeve 2013
© Copyright Andrew Campbell 2013

Published by: The Darsham Parochial Church Council

Sold in aid of All Saints' Church Fabric Fund
ISBN No: 978-0-9536592-3-4

All rights reserved. No part of this publication may be reproduced, stored in or introduced into a retrieval system, or transmitted, in any form or by any means (electronical, mechanical, photocopying, recording or otherwise), without prior permission of both the copyright owners and the publishers of this book.

Acknowledgements & sources, in addition to those mentioned in the text:-
Suffolk Record Office, Ipswich.
Lambeth Palace Library
Church of England Record Centre
British Library
N.R.A., Kew
Sheila Hardy - 'The Village School' (1979).
David Gooderham - 'Round by Will's Mother's Way'. (2000).
Royal Archives, Windsor Castle
Margaret Gomersall - 'The Elementary Education of females in England 1800-1870' with particular reference to Rural Norfolk & Suffolk. (London PhD thesis, 1991).
Nicholas D. Sign - The Reorganisation of Secondary Education in Suffolk 1900-1939 (UEA PhD Thesis, 2004).
Mary Sturt - The Education of the People. (1976).

Cover Picture: Darsham School pupils - 1928. Teachers - Miss Ashwell & Miss Lamb

CONTENTS

	Page
Introduction	1
Chapter 1 – Education, Education, Education	3
Chapter 2 – The Day Begins 1854 - 1877	9
Chapter 3 – Would they come. Would they learn?	22
Chapter 4 – The Struggles of Rural Education 1887 - 1900	32
Chapter 5 – Mr Ludbrook rules - OK! 1901 - 1925	49
Chapter 6 – Making the Best of Things. 1925 - 1945	68
Chapter 7 – Winding Down	99
Chapter 8 – And Finally . . .	110
Postscript -	115

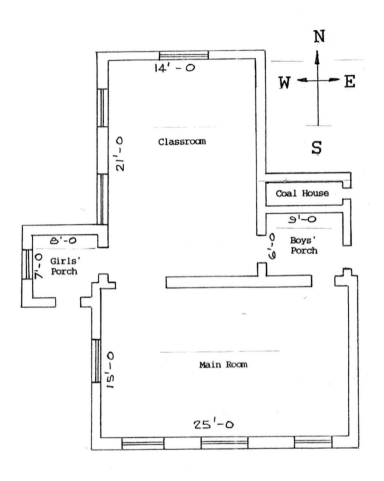

Plan of Darsham School

(Circa 1906)

Introduction

by Revd Canon Richard Ginn

Some years ago, a trilogy of books was proposed to commemorate the Millennium in Darsham. These books were more or less dependant upon the remarkable archive of Darsham history meticulously researched and recorded by Mrs Olive Reeve.

The first book was about one thousand years of the history of the church in Darsham. The second book was about one thousand years of the social and economic history of the parish. The third book was to be about the history of Darsham School.

Upon publication of the second book in 2008, Olive's thoughts immediately turned to the material that would be required for the writing of the third book but she sadly became ill and died before pen could be put to paper. The book is now completed and offered as a tribute to Olive, and it tells the story of a much loved local institution - our village school, sometimes in the words of those who attended there as children, and to them, thank you for sharing your experiences.

Olive's epitaph was "forever searching, forever learning." It would transform our society if we all undertook a commitment to life long learning. Our little village schools often succeeded in turning out fine citizens but it is one thing to learn as children and another thing to learn as adults.

We can reasonably hope that those who read these pages will have their memories of school days rekindled. May we all be reminded that we are all part of the story in the places where we have been in life, and that we all have the potential of adding our voices to the record of local history.

Whatever we learn or forget as children, we all need to ask questions as adults. Our curiosity should help to shape our futures. If we are "forever searching and forever learning," we can be changed and our society transformed.

Chapter One

Education? Education? Education?

In the British Isles, in the beginning of the nineteenth century, the national debate about basic education for all was slowing down. Given the wider background of the turbulence in Europe, people argued about whether education would build a more harmonious society, or whether it would feed a revolution. Some had a dream of unleashing a flowering of the human spirit; others worried that more of the fabric of the nation would be destroyed than would be renewed. Some hoped that education would equip the lower classes to be more useful; others feared that learning would sow the seeds of discontent.

Much of this preliminary thinking on educational outcomes centred on costs as well as results. As to costs, a lot of children doing the same thing organised by one teacher need not be expensive; tutors for individuals could remain the privilege of the upper classes. Results might best be achieved through repetition, learning by rote. It was realised that roof slates from demolished housing could provide an ideal recyclable writing surface for repeated practice. It was suggested that using older children to teach younger ones in a large class, under the leadership of a 'good' teacher worked better than having a greater number of lower quality teachers teaching smaller classes, perhaps graded by age or ability.

We can surmise that educating the poor would not have to cost too much. Children were expected to perform tasks well from memory, so understanding the underlying principles was not thought to be necessary.

However, despite some early philanthropic efforts at pioneering education among the poor such as Sunday Schools, there were continual arguments concerning funding. There were issues of accountability, regulation, religious affiliation and educational method. Debate postponed action. In such schools as existed (and let us not forget the ancient foundations such as choir schools and some grammar and public and preparatory schools, i.e. fee paying or endowment based institutions), there was no uniform pattern of discipline. One early educationalist, thinking of ways to discipline boys and teach cleanliness, thought that the answer was to send any boy who was dirty to have his face washed by the girls!

Whether the early nineteenth century schools were in town or country, the common background, at least for the smaller schools, was poverty. Generally these schools could not support a teacher who was qualified in any way. Teaching tended to be a secondary part of someone's livelihood.

Eventually discussions about education crystallised, but those who desired to establish mass education divided into two main factions, which came to be led by two different organisations. Both were founded in 1811. The Quaker and Nonconformist group became "The British and Foreign School Society", and the Anglican group became "The National Society for promoting the Education of the Poor in the Doctrine and Discipline of the Established Church" — it soon became known as 'The National Society'. The complicated social consequences of this division reverberated for many years.

Meanwhile, a countrywide survey of schools in 1816 yielded the report from Mr Mason, Curate at Darsham, that the village had a Sunday School for thirty children supported by voluntary contributions. It was a beginning for this small village near the east coast in Suffolk, but the pathetic inadequacy of this well-intended work is illustrated by the fact that between 1800 and 1819, three hundred and fifteen children were baptized in Darsham, so depending on the age range that this school catered for, perhaps only three out of every five of the child population in Darsham could possibly have been receiving any education at all, and that teaching was only for a few hours in a cold church on a Sunday! The poverty of Darsham, and the vulnerability that goes with poverty, is shown by the fact that in these years, fifty-three children died in the village. In addition five Darsham children died in the workhouse at Bulcamp.

Twenty-one years later in 1837 Mr Bond, Curate, applied for union with the National Society for Promoting Education of the Poor (etc.) on behalf of the

Sunday School at Darsham, but whether the school had been continuous during these years is not recorded; Sunday Schools could come and go as people were available to run them. Ten years later still, the National Society conducted the Church-School Inquiry 1846 - 1847, and the return from Darsham stated that: "There is no school in this parish, the children attending Yoxford National District School." Yoxford had a school with one paid Master teaching ninety-four boys, and one paid Mistress teaching seventy-seven girls, but it could be doubted whether many children from Darsham set foot in Yoxford School.

Darsham was not unusual as a village in Suffolk with no school. In 1818, there were six hundred and thirty-three parishes. Two hundred and sixteen of these parishes had no day school facilities. By 1833 the situation had improved though there were still one hundred and two Suffolk parishes without a day school, and forty-six of these did not even have a Sunday School. Where Sunday Schools existed, it can reasonably be assumed that Religion and the other three r's - Reading, wRiting and aRithmetic were all being taught.

One factor blocking the provision of education, readily identified during these years, was blatant local prejudice. Contemporary investigation found that many farmers were illiterate and were hostile to elementary education. Boys were seen as cheap labour to be deployed in the fields; they should not waste their time on unnecessary learning. Certainly education would encourage labourers to leave the land, and schooling would unfit men for work. The clergy colluded in this approach. For example, Charles Hughes, the Rector of Wixoe in Suffolk, wrote in 1819 that "those who are habituated early in life to regular labour generally turn out more useful and moral members of our society than those who were put to school too long." Presumably he excepted himself from this generalisation.

Sadly too, in many parts of Suffolk, there was little by way of subsidy from the National Society to help education rise from its sluggish beginnings. Such funds as were available tended to be directed to the emerging industrial districts, even though they came from the State and were meant for general distribution.

Meanwhile, if rural boys were destined for farm work, apprenticeships in family businesses, or work on the estates of the larger country houses, girls were regarded as being educated in their family units for marriage and motherhood, or for domestic service.

It is worth noting that in Darsham, both in 1816 and in 1837, it was a Curate who reported on the existence of the probably transient Sunday School. This was in the period, prior to parliamentary reform of the Church's structures, when a parson would hold a number of livings in plurality. William Kett was Vicar between 1789 and 1832 and was variously vicar of Shottesham and Waldringfield during this time. Vicar Weddall came to Darsham in 1832 but lived in Yoxford because the vicarage at Darsham was too dilapidated (owing to the prolonged absence of the previous incumbent).

Perhaps Darsham Sunday School was beneath the field of vision of these two men. Be that as it may, Christopher Mason, who was curate, in 1816 stated: "The poor are desirous of more sufficient means of education." *(House of Commons Papers 1819 ix)*. In his return of that year he reported a population of three hundred and eighty-seven, with forty-six poor persons, no education endowments available, but with a Sunday School of thirty children supported by voluntary contributions. The child population was rising. Four hundred and fifty children were baptised between 1820 and 1850, as against three hundred and fifteen for the previous twenty years. During the 1820 - 1850 period there were sixty-nine infant and child burials. There was a daily school in Darsham in 1835, but it only catered for twenty-five children, who were educated at the expense of their parents.

There was evidently no shortage of candidates for schooling, but perhaps a stable form of elementary education would only really dawn in Darsham with the arrival of a new vicar in 1851, the Reverend Mayhew, who was instituted in that year.

Chapter Two

The Day Begins
1854 - 1877

Various provisions for elementary education were being made, but not as yet in Darsham. There were National Schools, Ragged Schools, Workhouse Schools and Industrial and District Schools. Eventually they would become absorbed into the National State School system and renamed as Board Schools, each with a management board, regulated by the 1870 Act to provide Public Elementary Education.

In the absence of the provision of one or more of these kinds of schools, usually organised by those in a position of influence in a parish, working class children received either no education at all or, if they were lucky, basic instruction in the Three R's (Reading, wRiting & aRithmetic) at either a Sunday School, or a local Dame School. Dickens refers to Dame Schools in his novel 'Great Expectations' and they were a popular phenomenon in Victorian times. Common in England and colonial America, Dame Schools are believed to have existed from at least the 1500's until compulsory education in the 19th century. In Australia the first recorded school was a Dame School, started in 1789 in Sydney, where the children were taught by a female convict, Isabella Rossen. *(Source: Grigg, G. 2005 & the Statistical Society of London)*.

They were named 'Dame Schools' because they were often run by elderly women from their homes, catering for children up to the age of five years — at which age they were considered old enough to work. Unfortunately educational aims as well as attainment levels differed between schools. At the lowest level they were a form of child care, leaving parents free to work, but at some, as well as the basic three R's, pupils were taught skills such as sewing and knitting, skills which would help them in their later life, either in the home or in domestic employment. The method of teaching was 'parrot fashion' with the children repeating their lessons until they were learnt.

There are references to a Dame School in Darsham, but unfortunately no record of the location or the name of teacher(s). The only definite hard information we have comes from Kelly's Directory of 1846, when Miss Elizabeth Snell, the daughter of William Snell of Hill Farm, is recorded as being the local teacher. She was possibly the teacher at one of these daily schools that existed for a time as the need arose. Such a school had been running in Darsham in 1835.

Revd. Thomas Mayhew became Vicar in 1851, and the school (now the 'Old School House') was built as a day school in its earliest form at a cost of £80. At the time of the first Education Act in 1870, the next Vicar, the Revd John Thorp, described the school room as being built on ground belonging to the Parish on land left for Church purposes, but that there was no trust deed. He said that the school room measured 25 feet by 15 feet, and that the room stood 10 feet high to the wall-plate.

The first schoolmistress, Miss Matilda Maylam, started work in 1854. Then in 1857, Miss Charlotte Collings took up the challenge. She remained in post until 1877 when she had to leave because new regulations required her to be certificated. For a time, Miss Collings was assisted by her sister, Elizabeth, or Betsey. In 1872 it was recorded that Betsey was in charge of the infants, thirteen boys and five girls with an average age of four and a half years. Betsey was deaf, but it was reported that she was a competent teacher. Sadly, deafness was not her only problem and she ended her days in Melton Asylum, dying in 1881 at the age of 52, having been declared a lunatic. Charlotte and Betsey were daughters of Joseph Collings the wheelwright who lived in Low Road, Darsham, in the house called Lawn Cottage.

It would be impossible to obtain direct statistical evidence in the short term of changing behaviour of young people following the establishment of a school in Darsham, whether there was a flowering of the human spirit or the sowing of the seeds of discontent. However, there is interesting evidence of how juvenile crime was dealt with. Such reports can provide a flavour of the context of the lives of the young people involved. Local juvenile crime was reported in Suffolk newspapers. In April 1860, a "Juvenile Offence" was reported from the Yoxford Petty Sessions in the Ipswich Journal:

> "Frederick Edwards of Darsham was charged with having, on the 11th April at Darsham, feloniously stolen six eggs,

value three-pence, the property of James Blackman, and sentenced to seven days imprisonment in Beccles Gaol."

So there were issues surrounding the disciplining of the young in rural society. Another local "Juvenile Offender" was dealt with at Halesworth Court in September 1869:-

"Eliza Smith, alias Staff, late of Darsham, a juvenile of the age of 15 years, was brought up in custody of Sergeant Page, charged with having, on the 11th inst., at Blythburgh, stolen one Holland dress of the value of 12s., the property of James Yallop. Prisoner was sentenced to be imprisoned in Ipswich Gaol, and kept to hard labour for the space of two calendar months, and at the expiration of such imprisonment to be taken to Ipswich Reformatory School for the space of two years."

In isolation these reports might suggest that the children of Darsham were growing up in a society where the sticks were rather larger than the carrots, but there is evidence of a vigilance concerning the maltreatment of young people as well. This is illustrated by a report from Yoxford Court in November 1875:-

"William Catling, of Darsham, farmer, was

> charged with having, on the 5th November at Darsham, assaulted James Flegg, of the same place. This assault was not of a serious nature. Flegg, who is a juvenile, was in the service of Catling, and on the day named he struck and kicked him. He was fined 2s. 6d. and 8s.0d. costs, which he paid."

A differing aspect of the presence of the new schoolroom is presented by other newspaper reports from this period. These concern social events in Darsham. The schoolroom provided something that the village had never had before — neutral territory where all could meet. The accommodation was not large, but the schoolroom could now double as a village room. The earliest report of this development comes from an issue of the Ipswich Journal in January 1861:-

> "Through the kindness of Mr and Mrs Scrivenor the singers at the Church were liberally entertained at an evening party in the school-room a few weeks since..."

Again in January 1866, the schoolroom provided the opportunity for an occasion called "Penny Readings":-

> "The second series of penny readings, vocal and instrumental music, took place in the schoolroom on Wednesday evening last, and, though the weather

was very unfavourable, the room was well-filled in every part. The company appeared to enjoy extremely the programme before them, and frequently expressed by applause their approbation. The Misses Purvis, Mayhew, and Price acquitted themselves remarkably well on the piano. The Messrs Smythe, of Aldeburgh, again added considerably to the evenings amusement by their excellent singing. The readings were by A. Purvis, Esq., the Revd. T. Mayhew and Mr C.P. Jonas, and were well received and greatly appreciated by all."

Such reports can only be a tiny window opened on the interests and entertainments of our predecessors in Darsham. It is interesting to note that the talents required to bring off such an entertainment appear perhaps to have resided within the upper class of Darsham society at that time; the Purvis family of Darsham House, and the vicarage family and presumably their associates. Education for all, enabling a large cross section of society to acquire talent in this direction, still had its course to run. However, as far as Darsham School is concerned, the fact is that these events happened. It was not only the venue for the education of the young people, but the premises also functioned in the enhancement of village life.

Darsham School pressed on with the effort to educate

the children. At some time a Night School was established. In 1866, Revd John Thorp arrived to take up the duties of Vicar of Darsham. He soon realised that Darsham School was under resourced. In 1868, he applied to the National Society for a Book Grant. He declared that there were fifty children in ordinary attendance and that books were also needed for up to twenty-two Night Scholars. He listed the weekly fees. Older children had to pay two pence per week, while the younger children paid one penny per week. Night Scholars paid half a penny a week. He set out the annual school accounts:-

Income:	£.	s.	d.
Subscriptions and donations	16	1	6.
School Pence	10	5	0.
Endowment	4	0	0.
	£30	6	6.

Expenditure:	£.	s.	d.
Salary of Teacher	26	0	0
Books & Apparatus	10	0	0
Cleaning & Fire Lighting	1	0	0
Coal & Rent	2	3	0
Balance	0	13	6.
	£30	6	6.

Vicar Thorp added that the Parish was very poor, and that "we want about £2 or £3 of Books &c., and without some aid we must do without the books which would hinder the usefulness of the school." The National Society awarded a grant of £2.

Despite this rather meagre response by the National Society to the financing of education in Darsham, the government of the time now recognised that there was a national problem. Voluntary education as meted out by such bodies as the National Society had failed. Many of the nation's children were woefully ignorant, and in an increasingly industrialised nation this would lead to a shortage of skilled labour, and economic disaster.

In 1870, a new Act to provide for Public Elementary Education became law in spite of the opposition from among other factions, the established Church, which wished to retain influence over the nation's youth. There was a fear of indoctrination expressed on all sides.

The new Act provided that wherever school accommodation for the education of children was insufficient, a School Board should be elected by the ratepayers of the district, with authority to build and maintain Board Schools at the expense of the Ratepayers. The School Board had the powers to enforce school attendance. Darsham School became one of these Board Schools.

Attendance however, remained voluntary. Sadly for many families in Darsham, as well as across the country as a whole, children were an essential part of the workforce and generated significant income. Even if they attended school, and for many attendance was irregular, they still had to work to help the family scrape a subsistence in addition to the hours that they spent in school   Indeed, in towns there was widespread non-attendance. Even so it was not until 1880 that attendance at school was made compulsory from the age of five until the age of ten, and it was only in 1904 that employment of children before six in the morning and after nine at night was prohibited.

The Agricultural Gangs Act of 1867, regulating the employment of women and children in agricultural gangs, may also have ameliorated conditions for village children, and perhaps allowing a period in which younger children could attend school. It stipulated that no child under the age of eight was to be employed in an agricultural gang. The Act also required gang-masters to be licensed, but no doubt local farmers would have found the means of avoiding legislation that hindered the employment of cheap labour to any extent.

Now as soon as the 1870 Act to provide Public Elementary Education became law, Vicar Thorp applied to the National Society again, this time for a grant for an extension to the schoolroom. He felt that the existing school could only cater for forty-six children, and that room was needed for seventy-five. He proposed a twenty feet by fifteen feet extension for an estimated cost of £75. The National Society (still run by the Church of England, and funded by the State to provide education for the poor) awarded a grant of £10.

The 1870 Act established an Education Department with

powers to inspect schools. Darsham School was inspected in 1872. The Inspection Report said that there had to be room for eighty-one children. It stated that the schoolroom was deficient in that it was narrow with a brick floor, and that the walls were thin and damp. It was noted that the school had no proper desks or furniture, in other words children must have had to sit on the floor, and that there was not even a toilet. The comment was added, "There is surplus accommodation in Westleton, where there is a good school under a Master within reasonable distance. Boys at a certain age would attend school in that parish with advantage." Perhaps it is to be expected that an inspector arriving from afar might not perceive the prohibiting effect of the distance between two villages and of local rivalry.

In June 1875, the Education Department served notice that within six months, Darsham School had to be "enlarged to accommodate eighty-one children, and the floor of the existing schoolroom boarded as was proposed in 1870 and 1871, and parallel desks provided, and a certificated teacher appointed."

In January 1876, Vicar Thorp mentioned in a letter to the Education Department that a new schoolroom had been provided, and he asked for Miss Collings to be certificated. A further letter of January 1877 reported that the floor had been boarded, and desks and a toilet provided. However, despite her long service, there was no certification forthcoming for Miss Collings, and she had to leave in March 1877. Charlotte Collings finished her days in a house in Brussels Green, dying in 1896, at the age of 77 years.

The Vicar's effulgent speech at her farewell to the school is quite revealing of her role and of what was expected of education in our village. The following report was carried in the Ipswich Journal of Saturday 17th March 1877:-

DARSHAM SCHOOL

"At a meeting held in Darsham School, on Friday the 9th March, a presentation of £10 was made to Miss Collings as a token of the parishioners' appreciation of her long service as schoolmistress in the above parish. Miss Collings is leaving on account of the Government regulations requiring a certificated mistress. The vicar, the Rev. John Thorp made the presentation in these words:- "Dear Miss Collings, - In the midst of regrets at the circumstances which have necessitated a rupture of that union which has existed for upwards of 19 years between you, this school, this parish, and the managers of this school, one pleasing duty falls to my lot, as vicar of this parish and as manager of this school. It is that of presenting to you a small token of our great esteem of the way in which you have conducted this school during the many years you have held the responsible office of schoolmistress. When I look round on the children now in our school-room, I see some there the children of parents whom as children you educated years ago. This is a circumstance which falls to the lot of few teachers. During these years (ten only of which I have laboured with you), through good report and evil report, you have kept the even straightforward path of duty before you, and those duties have been discharged to the satisfaction of the managers, and to the thorough education of many in this school, some of who have left us, having, under you, attained a proficiency in various branches of education much to your credit. The greater part of such an education should and has better fitted them for the discharge of those duties which fall to their lot in that station of life to which in God's providence they have been called. Especially must I mention the needlework done in this school. We stand, according to the Government Inspector's report, very high, and in no school does he know of better work. How important this is I need hardly to point out. To this school we look for our future servants. To this school we look for the future mothers of future generations. What is a wife who cannot make her husband's shirt, or his clothes? This you have endeavoured to teach those under you, and with a very commendable amount of success. While offering you this token of our respect and appreciation of your work, we must offer what you will still more value, our hearty thanks for your labour of love amongst us and our very best wishes for the future. He who has upheld you hitherto will still uphold you. You have seen many ups and downs, many changes and chances amongst us, but He has never changed - the same yesterday, today, and for ever - and so you will find Him to the end of your days the same ever watchful God and Father, reconciled to us by the precious blood of Christ our Saviour, ever pouring on us every good gift from above, and His good gift the gift of the Holy Spirit.   I regret that our old and respected squire, Mr. Purvis, nor any of his family are able to be present with us, a regret which is mutually shared. I will only add that the spirit in which I have been met in this appeal gives the greatest proof of the estimation in which your services have been and are held; all have readily contributed. Wishing you every success for the future, we beg you to accept this token of our respect and esteem and hearty thanks for all your labours as schoolmistress in our village school."

Chapter Three

Would they come?   Would they learn?

By 1880, all children had to be at school until aged ten, but in towns there was generally a shortage of schools, and in the villages, though many now had schools, there was a persistent shortfall in attendance.

In the East Anglian countryside there was an extra impediment, which meant that boys were less likely to go to school. There was a long established custom among employers that a man was expected to be accompanied at work by his sons, sometimes as soon as they had reached their sixth birthday. If the man declined to bring them to work, in some places he could expect to be dismissed. It is impossible to investigate the extent of this practice, and it probably varied from trade to trade, and on the land, from farm to farm. However, given the force of local custom, it is quite possible that if this phenomenon persisted in Darsham until this period, there would be some delay in adjusting to regulations. The absence of court cases concerning boys' non-attendance might suggest that absence amongst boys was even being overlooked.

Now the interesting thing is that there are charges relating to girls' non-attendance. Joseph Lame, of Darsham was accused at Saxmundham Magistrates' Court in 1884 with having neglected to send his child (a daughter) to school. He was fined sixpence with two shillings costs.

John Smith of Darsham faced the same charge at Saxmundham in 1883, and was also fined six pence with two shillings costs. In 1884, John Smith was prosecuted on a repeat charge and was then fined sixpence with two shillings and six pence costs. Occasional criminal proceedings against parents for keeping their children away from school did not necessarily solve the problem of irregular attendance.

None-the-less the battle for the minds of the children continued. This battle was made all the more difficult because education was target driven. Each year a national education 'Code' was issued. The Code determined what was to be taught for each year of age, and what the children would be examined in, when the inspector called. After the inspector's visit, the grant that the school would receive for the following year was linked to the assessment of the school's performance in the Inspector's Report. Teachers' pay tended to be linked to the grant, and to school attendance.

In small rural schools the result was that the staff were burdened with totally unrealistic expectations. This letter from the teacher at Peasenhall School, published in the Ipswich Journal on 13th May 1882, illustrates the problem:

ELEMENTARY EDUCATION.

"Sir, If I were to go to Darsham Station, the nearest railway station to me, and on the arrival of a train I were to ask the driver to carry me to Norwich at the rate of 120 miles an hour, I might possibly get a reply similar to the following:-

"My engine has been constructed to travel at a certain rate. One hundred and twenty miles an hour is altogether beyond that rate, but if you wait here until I return, I will carry you to Melton at the rate of thirty miles an hour" I feel in the position of the engine driver. I have a certain task placed before me and I must earnestly consider whether or not I can accomplish it. At present I am using three sets of readers, including a set of geographical readers. When the Code of 1882 comes in force, I shall be compelled to have another set, historical readers. As I am the master of a rural school, my staff is necessarily limited, so that in future I shall have to make myself responsible for four standards - four to seven. I have carefully examined my reading books and I have made the following calculation of the number of lessons I alone shall have to give:- Reading lessons, 1,351; grammar lessons, 900; arithmetic lessons, 900; writing lessons, 900; composition or dictation lessons, 900; mental arithmetic lessons, 900; and singing from notes, 900. This gives a total of 6,751 lessons. Now, as there are fifty-two weeks in the year, seven of which we allow for holidays, it follows that there are just forty-five weeks, or 225 days, (five school days to a week), in which to prepare these lessons. By dividing the number representing the lessons by the number representing days, I find that I shall have to give at least thirty lessons each day in order to get through the work. There must be four hours secular work each day. Allowing thirty minutes for recess, there remains but three and half hours in which to give these lessons. By a sum in simple division I find that each lesson must last only seven minutes. But there is time always lost in changing lessons, so that the longest time a lesson will last will be about five minutes. It must not be forgotten, Sir, that our reading books are not compiled to amuse children. They are intended to instruct, so that they are literally crammed from beginning to end with technical lessons extracted from the works of our greatest thinkers and philosophers, and consequently require much patient explanation to make them at all to be understood by the children. I will leave it to your readers to judge how much intelligence an inspector can expect under such circumstances. The Code says that the pass for reading must be judged by "intelligence."

When I inform you that in addition to the above work, I must make myself responsible for the teaching of the lower standards, and the work of an assistant in the infants' room, it need not surprise you when I confess that I am looking forward to the future with very great misgivings. Please let it be borne in mind that I am not referring to schools in towns or others more favourably circumstanced. There are two ways of meeting my difficulty. First neglect grammar and geography, and confine my instruction to the three R's. In this case the character of the school may suffer, and there would be a loss of the Government grant for those subjects. Secondly, engage extra staff. This would entail heavier burdens on the ratepayers, who are already taxed beyond their means. We must all fully admit that the framers of the 1882 Code have laboured with a desire to place the education of the country on a sound basis. But, Sir, I have witnessed the introduction of all the Codes since 1862, and I have found that each year has brought about some alterations. I am afraid that the Code of 1882 will be no exception, as so long as nature is outraged in order to enable the Education Office to apply a money test, so long will there be cause for such annual alterations.

Each Code has been based on the supposition that every child has the same brain power. It assumes that a schoolmaster can supply what God has withheld, when it demands that every child shall perform a certain amount of mental labour at a certain age. Of all of the most ridiculous absurdities none can be greater than that which compels the schoolmaster to push all children into a higher class each year. Fit or unfit for the journey, he must go on. There must be no standing still. If an attempt be made to withhold children the merit grant may be withheld.

One of the objects of the Code, is to make every teacher an Arnold. But, Sir, who is to judge an Arnold from a commonplace teacher? How is he to be gauged? He cannot be gauged by the children present on the day of examination, but by those children who have left the school, and have been fighting the battle of truth and progress. Arnold was not judged so much by his resident pupils as by those whom he had prepared for the battle of life, and who had come out of the conflict triumphantly. If we teachers, under present circumstances, aim at the distinction of an Arnold, we are in danger of being painfully disappointed on the day of examination, when a small money grant may hold us up to ridicule and pity. Arnold was free, we are bound securely with red tape, so that we cannot move in any shape without permission of the Education Office. Had Arnold been bound as we teachers are, we should never have had his name dangled before us, and had Pestalozzi, Bell, Lancaster, and

Frobel been bound as we are, the world would have lost the examples of those great pioneers of enlightenment. Our sorrowful lot has been cast in a sordid and unscientific (educationally) age. Those pioneers studied the nature of children; we must study "results". They looked to the manhood of every child; our view is confined to the day of the examination, when we tremblingly examine the schedule, to see how much money we may put in our pockets.

    I am, yours faithfully,
    H. O'DONNELL."

Quite simply, however hard rural teachers worked, they could not succeed. The mechanisms of administration and regulation conspired to drive down achievement, all in the interests of meeting unattainable, and often pointless or useless targets.

Not surprisingly, Darsham School went through teachers at a rate of knots. Miss Collings was squeezed out of service in March 1877 (had she perhaps managed to sail her own sweet course regardless of the Code, and was that why she was never certified?). Between March 1877 and December 1887, when Mr Pybus arrived, the children endured fifteen other appointments. There could be no stability, and there would be little attraction for children attending a school that not even teachers seemed to want to attend.

The School Log Book tells the tale. In 1880 there were eighty children on the books, but the average attendance was forty-three. The then teacher's capacity was praised in the

Inspector's Report, but arithmetic and grammar were described a deplorably poor. The situation was little changed in 1881 when there were ninety children on the roll and the average attendance was fifty-two. The school grant was reduced because of deficient instruction in arithmetic, and the lack of proper privies for the infants. The Inspector's report of 1882 portrayed the teacher then at the school as 'culpably indifferent' and the school grant was further reduced. Darsham School was on a downward slide. Discipline and learning both suffered. Somehow things did get better and improvements were beginning to be noted after a further two years.

Numbers at the school were bound to fluctuate as large families moved around following the father and his work. In the middle of 1884, there were seventy-three children on the books, but 1885 began with only fifty-eight pupils. This changing state of affairs affected the school's income from the annual grant, and at this time parents were expected to contribute towards the costs of the school at a rate of a penny a week per child. Falling rolls meant fewer resources. In September 1885, the school managers resolved that any coming for the second week running without their penny should be sent home A steady income was crucial to the continual running of the school.

In December 1887 the school finally gained a valuable anchor. Mr Pybus was appointed headmaster, to be joined by Mrs Pybus in the following year as assistant mistress. Mr Pybus was to be in post for nearly five years, and immediately

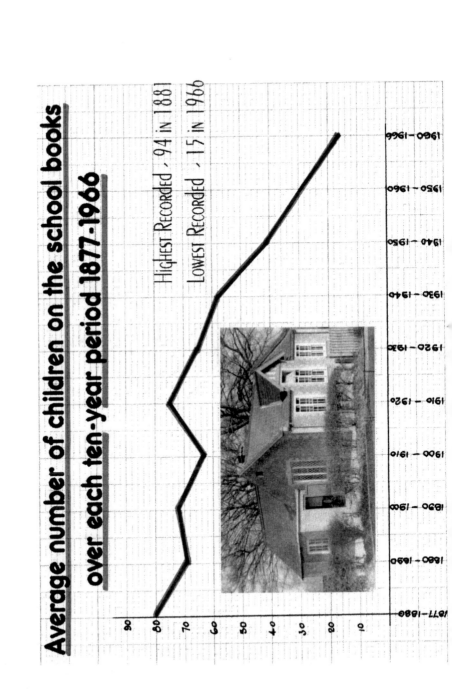

From Churchwardens' Accounts.

1869- probably from the School Board, rent of £1. 5s received for the school and garden and continued to be paid to the Darsham Churchwardens from the Education Committee until the school closed in 1966.

From time to time the schoolroom was rented out to various organisations for an agreed rental, for example:
1902/29 To the 'Sick & Burial Club' at 15/- p.a
1904   For a political meeting - 5/-
1905   For a political meeting - 5/-
1906   Rural Labourers' Union - 5/-
1909   For two Conservative Meetings - 10/-
1909   For two Radical Meetings - 10/-
1910   For an Election as a polling Station - 10/-
1921   To Mr Etheridge - possibly for a political meeting - 5/-
1922   For a political meeting - 5/-
1922   For R.D.C. Election Polling Station - 5/-

upon his appointment he began to make improvements.

In addition to the battle for minds, there was also an interesting and perhaps novel battle for hearts as well; a forerunner of the idea of bringing an ecological awareness to the centre of education. We can get a small insight into the hearts of a few Darsham children through a children's newspaper called "Little Folk." This paper ran from 1871 until 1935. In 1882, the magazine started the "Little Folks' Humane Society". Recruits were invited who would promise, "I ...., hereby undertake, as far as it lies in my power, to be kind to every living creature that is useful and not harmful to man." The membership list for this Humane Society closed in 1884, when it achieved 50,000 names, but not before three Darsham girls had signed up. Amongst the recruits listed in the issue for 1st January 1884, were Annie Mountain, aged 17 years and Laura Mountain, aged 14 years, both daughters of Henry Mountain, a builder, and his wife Eliza, of The Street, Darsham. Agnes Smith, aged 13 years signed as well. She was the daughter of George Smith, the blacksmith, and his wife Pamela, of The Forge, The Street, Darsham. Amidst the hardships of these times, it is a great credit to our village that three of our children felt that it was worth the trouble to make the declaration.

One last incident recorded in the Ipswich Journal for 17th January 1885 illustrates some perils of the time where the proper care of the young are concerned. One morning in the previous November, Amelia Mary Cullingford, aged 8 years, the daughter of Walter Cullingford, a horseman of Brussels Green, Darsham and his wife Mary, was left in the kitchen of her home with two younger siblings, whilst their mother went out for an hour. Alas, Amelia removed the fireguard and her dress caught fire. She was badly burned on her back and head before a neighbour intervened. Amelia was cared for at home until Christmas, when she was removed to Halesworth Hospital, where she died on 9th January.

Illness or accident took children away seemingly at random, though in fact it was usually in their infancy that they were most at risk. This table recording the incidence of death of children of Darsham between 1850 and 1889 does reveal a gradual decline in child deaths, and this in spite of a period of increasing birth rate, but it would not be until advances in public health and the control of disease had run its course that infant mortality would largely become a fear of the past.

Deaths of children in Darsham

	0 - 4 years	5 - 10 years
1850 - 1859	31	3
1860 - 1869	34	1
1870 - 1879	20	9
1880 - 1889	15	1

Broadly speaking, until this period of history was past, death among the young was accepted as a distressing fact, but as part of life. Large families ensured that a struggle was maintained, but the ever-increasing effects of a better educated population would eventually see the end of this grim aspect of life in England. Mr Pybus, headmaster, and Mrs Pybus as his assistant teacher, as well as future notable teachers of Darsham School would prove to be at the forefront of this change in our rural part of East Suffolk.

Chapter Four

The Struggles of Rural Education
1887 - 1900.

At this point, before plunging into the details of Darsham School life, it is worth stepping back briefly to note some interesting themes. Firstly, there was the question of how education was to be paid for. Not surprisingly, those who provided the money wanted to pay as little as possible. Secondly, there were the pressures of an ever evolving and enlarging curriculum. Thirdly, there was a conflict between the aspirations of those who wanted education to produce dutiful citizens of the Empire, and others who simply wanted to prepare children to be useful workers in East Suffolk. And fourthly, in the background, there were those who had ideals about children and society, who hoped to unleash the potential of each child with a view to renewing the life of the nation.

It is to be feared that few of the youngsters from Darsham went on to become achievers elsewhere. At this time, only four or five per thousand elementary school children had any hope of passing on to a grammar school. A rare note of merit appears in the Ipswich Journal of 7th February 1887:-

> "Richard Girling Arnott, of Darsham, a pupil at Beccles College, had gained special distinction in the last Diocesan examination in religious knowledge."

This boy was not Darsham born. He was the son of George Tacon Arnott, Corn & Coal Merchant and Maltster, in business near the railway station in Darsham. Richard Arnott's father was from Southampton; his mother was from Westleton.

However, to return to the details: Under Mr Pybus, who had arrived in December 1887, the boys were now to be taught Geography whilst the girls were doing their Needlework. The School Log Book reveals that in February 1888, older children were (not surprisingly) deplorably ignorant in Geography; they had no idea what an island or a cape looked like. In March 1888, it was noted that all but the simplest mental arithmetic was beyond the capacity of the children. However, satisfactory progress was being made in singing by note. It was also noted that Samuel James; Chester Smith; Charlotte Smith and Nelson Smith were deplorably ignorant through lack of attendance (the Smith family of the court case of 1894 again?) Perhaps Mr Pybus was tempted to despair of the uphill struggle of education in Darsham? In 1888 he recorded that: "It seems a hopeless task to change their minds from the almost chaotic darkness which prevails during this year."

Even so there was progress, and there was encouragement. In the Ipswich Journal for 7th December 1888 it was recorded about Darsham Board School that:- This school was examined a short time ago, and passed 90 per cent. The following report has been received from H.M.'s Inspector:- "This school promises well. The standards and infants are classed as good. Geography and sewing are fair; English is good; singing by note good. Bricked pathways to and from the school would be a great improvement without much outlay." The total grant exceeds that for the last year by £4 13s 3d.

The strange system of payment by results, which ensured fewer resources for under-achieving schools, was now, at last, being harnessed to recognise the improvement in Darsham School.

Issues of discipline emerged in 1889. It seems that Charles Stammers, whose father was a carpenter on the Darsham House Estate, living at Lodge Cottage, Low Road, twice stepped beyond Mr Pybus's powers of patience. On the first occasion, the boy had three strokes on his posterior. A subsequent note from his mother complained that the headmaster had 'thrashed him severely.' Mr Pybus recorded in the School Log Book, "I asked her to show me the marks. There was one short mark about 1" long resembling a scratch and I asked the Rev. Clarke to look. He said that it was very little and that the boy had not been punished severely." Mrs Stammers sent another note withdrawing the charge.

The second time, Master Stammers was joined by Walter Cullingford, of the family living at Brussels Green, mentioned in the last chapter. Both boys were caned for attempting truancy. This time, Mr Pybus recorded, "The latter boy's mother came to the school in a most insolent manner. She showed me two marks on his posterior. I have not the slightest regret about this as the punishment was administered in a calm, deliberate manner and was richly deserved."

Perhaps it is an unfair link to make, but the complaint was made by Mrs Cullingford, who had left three of her youngest children alone at home for an hour four years previously with tragic consequences for Amelia, the child left in charge.

The H.M.I. report for 1889 stated that there had been a gratifying improvement in our pleasant school, where indications of capable and energetic teaching abound. The Inspector commented that more might be achieved if less were attempted, but no guidance was given as how or in which parts, the curriculum might receive less attention.

In 1890 the annual inspection report again remarked that with so many subjects to teach (because of enforced teaching to the national Code), the quality must suffer. This was a year that began and ended with poor attendance. At the start of the year there was sickness. There had been heavy snow in March, when work got behind, and at the end of the year there was such severe weather that on one day there were only sixteen children at school. Even so, there were compliments in the annual inspection report. The poor weather and low attendance continued through January and February of the following year but this could well have prevented the spread of the highly infectious disease, Meningitis.

On 17th February, the following was recorded in the school's Log Book:

"An unusual and melancholy event happened in the village this morning. One of the school children has died of meningitis after an illness of three weeks. He was one of the sharpest and most intellectual boys in the school."

The Burial Register of the Parish Church noted him as Harry Percy Staff, aged 9, choirboy of the Parish Church. Harry, whose baptismal name was actually Harold Percy, was the son of Henry Staff, a Mole Catcher of Cheney Green, Darsham and his wife Maria.

For many years the Log Books recorded the poems that the different age groups were required to learn by direction of the national Code. In 1891, the older children were expected to learn the first one hundred and fifty lines from Milton's poem 'Comus.' This stately fantasy from 1634 begins with a sentence that lasts eleven lines:-

> Before the starry threshold of Jove's Court
> My mansion is, where those immortal shapes
> Of bright aerial spirits live ensphered
> In regions mild of calm and serene air,
> Above the smoke and stir of this dim spot,
> Which men call earth, and, with low-thoughted care.
> Confined, and pestered in this pinfold here,
> Strive to keep up a frail, and feverish being
> Unmindful of the crown that virtue gives
> After this mortal change, to her true servants

Darsham Pupils - c. 1895/1900

Darsham Pupils - c. 1912/1914

Parochial Returns - LOCAL SCHOOLS - Survey of 1816

Information supplied by parish clergy giving details of Sunday Schools, National, British & Dame Schools.
PRO Ref: HC 1819 ix [House of Commons Papers]

	DARSHAM Christr. Mason Curate.	WESTLETON Daniel Packard Vicar	MIDDLETON Daniel Packard Rector	DUNWICH No officiating Minister	YOXFORD Henry Whittington Curate
Population	387	713	564	208	1007
Poor in 1815	46	72	43	19	107
Particulars relating to endowments for the education of youth	None	None	None	None	None
Other institutions for purpose of education	Sunday School for 30 children supported by voluntary contributions	None	None	None	Sunday School principally supported by the Curate attended by 130-172 children; 3 Boarding schools; 5 Day schools for 68 poor children
Observations	The poor are desirous of more sufficient means of education	As Darsham	As Darsham	As Darsham	Poor manifestly without means of giving their children better education than that which the Sunday School affords and many children forget in the weekdays, what they learned on the Sabbath.

Amongst the enthroned gods on sainted seats.

What the children made of it all is not recorded, but they must have looked with envy at the lines of 'The Miller of Dee' that were set for the next youngest group.

On 2nd January that year, the Ipswich Journal had reported that George Holmes; Abraham Smith; Joseph Lane and Clara Newson all of Darsham were charged before Saxmundham Petty Sessions with not having caused their children to attend school. (The poem set for the older children this year was to be Goldsmith's 'The Deserted Village'). Douglas Parry-Crooke of Darsham House was one of the magistrates on the bench that day. Newson's case was withdrawn; Holme's and Lane's cases were adjourned and only Abraham Smith was convicted and fined six pence with three shillings costs. Was Mr Parry-Crooke adopting the role of the village defender?

On 9th April 1892, it was reported by the Ipswich Journal that Mr A.J. Swinburne H. M. Inspector, had examined the scholars of Darsham Evening School and complimented them on their knowledge of history. In 1892 the Evening School was probably held at the premises now called Shingle Cottage in The Street, Darsham. During this period it catered for adults learning subjects for the City & Guilds examinations, a set of examinations that had emerged as an examination system of national standing from the middle of the 19th century onwards. The Evening School was to continue until about 1919, being run from 1902 by the East Suffolk Education Committee.

Meanwhile, poverty and illness continued to shadow Darsham children, though two girls had returned to Darsham School after a spell in the workhouse. In May 1892 it was sadly recorded that Emma Ashford, a daughter of Charles Ashford, coachman at the big house, had died in London. In June, the school was closed for a time because of an outbreak of mumps— eighteen children were infected in one week.

St Vitus Dance is a neurological condition more common in children than adults, and also more common in girls than in boys. The commonest cause is from a previous infection of a particular type of Streptococcus bacterium. The patient loses control of, usually, all limbs. Movement is uncontrollable except in sleep. There can be facial contortions and uncontrollable tongue movements. Commonly the symptoms persist for about six months, but the condition can last for as long as two years.

Entries in Darsham School Log Book record how it affected Annie Read's schooling. Annie was one of the large family of Daniel Read, a farm labourer, and his wife Laura of High Street, Darsham. She was born in 1885, and in 1892 at the age of seven years, she was found to have St Vitus Dance. She returned to school in May, after a protracted bout of illness and "was to be treated with the greatest care and not spoken to harshly or to be troubled to learn." Again two years later, on 1ˢᵗ June 1894 Mr Ludbrook, the then headmaster, noted that Annie Read was re-admitted to school. She had made a partial recovery and was admitted to Standard 1. It was suggested that it would be inadvisable to press her or she may have a relapse.

'Dr. Williams' Pink Pills for Pale People' was a well-known patent medicine of the time. It was publicised as a cure for St Vitus' Dance with a clever style of copy writing in many newspapers. You were not aware that you were reading an advertisement, rather the effects of the pills was publicised as a news item. Annie Read was taken up as an example of a miraculous cure by the power of the pink pills, and the advertisement appeared on 20th March 1895 in newspapers such as Bristol Mercury & Daily Post; Belfast News-letter; Derby Mercury, and on Thursday 21st March 1895 in the Northern Echo, and again on Sunday 24th March 1895 in Reynolds Newspaper:

"**A Demonic Saint**. Saint Vitus has rather the repute of demon than saint, St. Vitus' dance being the special scourge of childhood. It may not be generally known that St. Vitus' dance, and all nervous disorders of children and adults, are easily cured by a very simple plan. A little girl at Darsham, Suffolk, Annie Read, who was sixteen weeks in bed with St. Vitus' dance, her arms and legs twisting and moving so that she used to roll out upon the floor, was cured in a fortnight (as the mother and Mr T. Neville, Scripture reader, Darsham, told a reporter) by *Dr. Williams' Pink Pills for Pale People.* The same medicine cures and prevents Influenza in children and adults, and cures rheumatism, sciatica, neuralgia, paralysis, locomoter, ataxy, nervous headache, scrofula, chronic erysipelas, and sallow complexion. Dr. Williams' Pink Pills are a specific for the female sex. In men they cure all cases from worry, overwork, or excesses. Sold by Dr. Williams' Medicine Company, 46, Holborn Viaduct, London, and by chemists at 2s. 9d. a box, or six boxes 13s. 9d., post free. Only genuine in pink wrapper with full name: *Dr. Williams' Pink Pills for Pale People.*"

In fact the pills were marketed in no less than eighty-two countries illustrated by a series of case histories such as that of Annie Read. One must hope that the girl's parents were financially rewarded for this particular advertisement, which appeared in newspapers even as far away as Australia. Mary Baillie, a pupil of Darsham School (now Mary Felgate of New South Wales) has seen the advertisement in an archived Australian newspaper while she was engaged on other research. However, it would be wrong to claim that Dr Williams' Medicine Company, purporting to be of 46, Holborn Viaduct, London, represents an entrepreneurial commercial enterprise fostered by the advances of education in Great Britain. The company was in fact the trading arm of the Canadian company of G.T. Fulford & Co creating huge wealth for its proprietor, the Ontario born philanthropist George Taylor Fulford.

On 23rd August, 1892, Mr Pybus had recorded in the Log Book of Darsham School: "Today I give up charge of this school. The only thing that I regret about leaving Darsham is that I must leave such a nice set of scholars." It seems that he preferred the children of Darsham to the adults, and he does seem to have done wonders for their education. He took up a new appointment at Theberton.

The new headmaster, Mr Waller, arrived from Hartlepool. Standards deteriorated. Mr Waller survived just over a year until December 1893. His grounds for resignation were that he claimed that he did not care for a mixed school. However, two things were worthy of note for 1893: the first was that the school leaving age was raised to eleven years. Perhaps just as important as that was the fact that the school now received a new headmaster who was to stay for twenty-five years. Mr & Mrs Ludbrook provided great stability both for the school and the village.

The Inspector's Report for 1893, the year in which Mr Waller was headmaster, had indicated deterioration in the life of the school. Mr Ludbrook noted the disorder in the school and that it was impossible to find enough books from which to read. He set to work to reorganise the curriculum. The older children were now going to cover world geography 'as scarcely anything is known about it.' By February 1894 the Managers were stating that it would be impossible to squeeze any more time into the timetable because inspection requirements had to be met, and the Vicar had to be refused his application to be allowed to give Scripture lessons once a week. Raising the school leaving age of course made a difference to the numbers on the roll. By the end of 1894 there were eighty on roll and the school grant was raised to £58. 5s. 0d. The previous year it has been only £44. 2s. 6d.

During 1894 the struggles with illness continued. There are reports in the Log Book of ringworm, and an epidemic of whooping cough. Annie Read's sporadic attendance due to St Vitus' Dance has already been mentioned. A sadder detail of the effects of illness on a family and its siblings is also recorded for that year. James Mayhew was absent through illness. He was the son of George Mayhew, a farm labourer, living in Darsham Street. James was described as the most promising boy in the top form. On 19th April, it was recorded that James was very ill at home, with little prospect of recovery. His sister, Nellie, aged 11 years, was having to stay at home to look after him, so she was making no progress with her schooling during this time and a younger sister, Rose, aged 7 years, was noted as making no progress in sewing and knitting. Alas, James' death was recorded on 23rd April. The church burial register describes him as aged 14 years, a choirboy.

This death is reminiscent of the death of Harold Percy Staff, which had happened three years previously. Had the two boys lived, could they have raised the fortunes of the poor families in the next generation as the direct result of being better educated than their parents? This was the hope expressed for the cause of mass education by a significant few.

In James Mayhew's case we do know of an immediate effect of his death on his sisters. They were evidently having difficulty adjusting to their brother's death. Nellie was reported for absence during June and Rose was caned for lying. Towards the end of the year the Log Book records bad weather. It was November.

Over the next two years a familiar pattern of sporadic absenteeism continued. One girl, Jessie Dunnett, was caned twice for persistently talking. Influenza, measles, coughing and other diseases came and went. In July 1895 it was noted that many of the children were absent, helping with the hay. At other times children were reported away, carrying food to their fathers working in the harvest fields. There was also regular absenteeism for stone-picking, looking after pigs, gleaning, rabbiting and rat-catching.

In the meantime the pressures on schools in Suffolk reached headlines in the Ipswich Journal. An interesting insight is offered in the edition of 6th October 1894:

Suffolk Teachers in Council
Our Education System Condemned.
A large gathering of managers, teachers, and others interested in education assembled at Lowestoft, on Saturday afternoon, under the auspices of the National Union of Teachers, the meeting included members of the Norwich, Gt. Yarmouth,

Yoxford and Waveney Valley Teachers Associations. The Mayor of Lowestoft presided. Mr F .B. Gale, referring to the overburdened curriculum, said that there had been a lessening of the curriculum. All subjects were more or less increased in difficulty, and far greater results were expected now than before, and more subjects were made compulsory. He was desirous of giving every child A THOROUGHLY COMPREHENSIVE EDUCATION, but many of the subjects now taught or contemplated he condemned as utterly useless. Mr T.J. Macnamara pointed out how the curriculum became heavier and heavier as each successive Minister of Education added their own particular methods, without taking anything away. He next alluded to what he termed "the abominably close" manner in which teachers were supplied with school materials, and how abominably the children were overworked. Under the present system there was no time for any moral instruction to be imparted. Teachers desired most anxiously the perpetuation of the Scripture lesson. Education had become commercialised, and the Union wanted the help of the school managers, particularly clergymen, in its endeavour to break down the payment by results system. He condemned the niggardly salaries doled out to teachers by the State, and stated that while the LOWEST WAGES OF POLICEMEN IN SUFFOLK was 20s. 5d. a week, there were some certificated head masters in the county who were receiving less than £1 weekly. There should be greater fixity of tenure with teachers."

It would be difficult to go further without mentioning the

school inspector of the times, H.M. Inspector of Schools, Mr Alfred James Swinburne. He was a regular visitor to Darsham school. Many of his visits were unannounced. He was quite a popular figure amongst teachers, as shown by the report from the Ipswich Journal of 11th July, 1896:-

EDUCATION IN SUFFOLK.
ADDRESSES BY Mr. SWINBURNE.

"Mr A.J. Swinburne, H.M. Inspector of schools for East Suffolk District, on Saturday addressed the teachers of the Yoxford and District branch of the N.U.T. at Saxmundham, over which Mr George Pybus (Theberton) presided. Having referred to the splendid new schools at Friston, Somerleyton and Lowestoft, Mr Swinburne said all could be congratulated on the educational advances made in the district, an advance which was general and all along the line, and he was pleased to be able to record in the last Blue Book that the chains of good schools throughout the district were rapidly becoming complete, there being comparatively few links missing. He felt all must feel pleased that the beneficent value of education was so generally and fully recognised. He impressed upon the teachers the importance of pauses in reading, comparing fast reading without pauses to a hungry man having a dish of soup poured over his mouth and head all at one time, comparatively little having time to enter. In writing, the style was certainly a matter for the teachers to consider, so long as each system was taught on its merits, though he was not so strongly prepared to support the so-called upright and similar styles as he had been, the modifications in the style often being great factors in its value. The practice of using fingers in counting in arithmetic and in pointing during reading he strongly deprecated, and he again impressed upon the teachers the value of placing the ball frame on a stand instead of carrying it about the class. Object lessons were still often unsuitable for the locality, such lessons as those on a church tower and a hedgehog being more homely to children. The method and matter column in the notes of lessons for young children were not nearly so important as the judicious selection of the chief heads on which the lessons could be built. The poetry for recitation was still often unsuitable and morbid, some of the lighter, brighter, short poems from the American poets being very suitable. The spread of evening schools was very gratifying, comparatively few of the important towns and villages now being without these useful factors in education."

Mr Swinburne left a book called *"Memories of a School Inspector - Thirty-five years in Lancashire and Suffolk." (Published in Saxmundham in 1912).* Whilst he forbears to mention Darsham by name, he did write that, "the main obstacle popular education has to overcome was a prejudice on the part of well-meaning farmers, and the landed interest generally .... against the diffusion of knowledge." *(Page 69).* He recalled one small rural school board complaining to its newly elected member, the Vicar, "Since you've been appointed, we can't get the stones gathered." *(Page 86).* Swinburne noted the frequent pressures which excluded clergy, who were often the only university educated person in

Prize Scheme Award

Mr & Mrs Ludbrook (Marked X)

a community, from influence on our village schools.

When he arrived in Suffolk, Mr Swinburne had found that there was no forum for the exchange of ideas and recipes for good practice between teachers. His innovations must have forwarded ideas about good practice in education considerably, as well as raising the profile of education among the general population of East Suffolk. He chose to use methods to advance educational standards that were very different from the target-orientated efforts of the yearly Codes issued by the Education Office. He established a circulating library for teachers. He also established an annual competition known as the East Suffolk Prize Scheme. The idea was for schools to submit pupil's work to the competition, for which prizes to the individual pupils would be awarded. Certificates were issued which could be displayed in schools. Teachers would also see each other's work, and could interact, discuss and learn from each other. Over the years, the Ipswich Journal reported the main prizes awarded at the competitions.

In 1892, on October 8th, very shortly after Mr Pybus had resigned as headmaster of Darsham School, the school was first mentioned with the award of 'highly commended for a stocking, crafted by F. Ellenger.' This girl was Flora Ellinger, aged 10 years. Flora and four siblings lived with their grandparents in The Street, but her grandfather was a grocer & draper, her grandmother a draper's assistant and her aunt a dressmaker. Perhaps Flora had a slight advantage in this particular competition. However, four years later when the school was once more improving under the tutelage of Mr and Mrs Ludbrook, it was recorded that on 31st October 1896 the second prize for a chemise had been awarded to Annie Smith from Darsham School. Again in 1898 Darsham Board School came equal first for a 'day shirt' and Annie Smith came third for 'Senior Girls' Darning' (an old stocking). Rose Mayhew was obviously working well once more because she came third in the competition for a knitted vest for a child of six. Further needlework prizes were recorded in 1900. Alice Flowers, aged 10 years, from Priory Farm, Darsham, received first prize for a chemise.

The Annual Exhibition of the Scheme had by this time expanded. In 1898 there were swimming competitions, boy's writing and drawing, and girl's writing competitions were also included. There were also demonstrations of best practice in teaching a class, on which teachers could model their own lessons. There were music competitions.

It must have been a comfort to Mr & Mrs Ludbrook that 1900 ended with the H.M.I.'s report that "the children are receiving an excellent training." Then four years later, in 1904, Darsham School children really excelled in the annual exhibition of the Scheme. A copy of the certificate that was issued to the school has survived and is shown in this volume.

Despite the struggle, Darsham School was coming out on top.

Chapter Five

Mr Ludbrook rules - OK!
1901 - 1925

The Edwardian era, the period between 1901 and 1910, is usually portrayed as being a period of golden years of prosperity, stability and elegance, even though problems for ordinary people continued with large families living in bad housing, oppressed by hard work, and financial struggle.

In Darsham there was the benign influence of the Parry Crookes with the annual treat at Darsham House for the village children. There were also annual Sunday School outings organised by the staff and by the vicarage, and similar outings organised by the Darsham Methodist Chapel. With the 1900 Census revealing that there were a hundred and fifteen children in the village aged twelve or under (thirty percent of the total population of three hundred and seventy-nine), these two occasions must have been quite something.

There were village suppers in the schoolroom, where nowadays village people were taking part in the entertainment, perhaps suggesting a higher general level of education in the population as a whole. The Halesworth Times of 3rd May 1904 reports a supper organised by the Darsham Church congregation "for all the old people of the age of 65 years and upwards."

> "After the supper whilst the old men were enjoying their pipes and ale, an entertainment took place, presided over by Mr J. Norton, Churchwarden. The following assisted: Mrs Norton, Messrs. Simpson Bros., Miss Arnott, Miss Fisher, Miss Tennant, the Rev. Dr. Tennant."

For Darsham School itself there was a participation in the East Suffolk Prize Scheme, and the school was now enjoying a period of excellence. From this period we have the earliest surviving Darsham School exercise book, the work of Harold Aldrich. The book begins with the beautifully copied words of 'Home, Sweet Home,' followed by the first two verses of Psalm 90:

> Lord, thou hast been our dwelling place in all generations, before the mountains were brought forth, or even thou hadst formed the earth and the world, even from everlasting thou art God.

Reading the summary report of H.M.I. Swinburne in the Log Book for 1909, the school comes across as a time in the children's lives when they were well occupied in learning and they were obviously producing excellent work. They must have been happy and content in a safe environment in the school under the resourceful influence of Mr and Mrs Ludbrook.

Instruction: "The school maintains a high standard of efficiency. The instruction characterised by exceptional originality. Amongst other points calling for praise may be mentioned needlework and freehand drawing - the latter being largely based on nature study. In scale drawing, the boys make their own rough sketches and measurements of the objects and reproduce them accurately and neatly. Hand writing is good and composition making sound progress. Physical exercises are satisfactorily taught."

"Thrown on his own resources by having to teach five to six standards singlehandedly, the schoolmaster has solved the problem by self-help and has, so to speak, instead of one monitor, a school of monitors teaching themselves. His success is such as to surpass that achieved in many schools more liberally staffed. He has succeeded in showing not so much as what he can do with as what he can do without - an important maxim these days. The infants are kindly and well taught."

From this extract it is worth noting as well, that the

curriculum still demanded development of technical abilities, sewing and needlework and scale drawing, and perhaps there was a greater emphasis on development of comprehension through composition. There was attention to physical fitness, and even a demand for the aesthetics as well as the awareness of the natural world through free drawing. The meanness of financial provision in education in Mr Ludbrook's school, produced one educational development which was way before its time: that of child-centred learning and utilisation of the help of older pupils. This was carried out under careful supervision. The older pupils used their own learning techniques to help the younger ones with theirs. It was a very different take on the monitoring system advocated by educationists at the beginning of the previous century, which only strengthened the dominance of rote learning as an educational method.

As to discipline, clearly Mr Ludbrook could achieve discipline without having to resort to draconian methods. In the Punishment Book for the years 1901-1914, several years could elapse with no recorded corporal punishment.

It is at this period that Early 20th Century Patriotism begins to emerge as a new theme linking 'Home and Empire', and it makes its appearance in connection with new ideas as to what constitutes a good elementary education. From 1907, comes the outline of the observance of Empire Day at Darsham School. Empire Day was celebrated on May 24th each year, that date being the birthday of Queen Victoria. The day's proceedings at school were reported as follows:

1. Children attended school and the register was marked.
2. The Union Flag was hoisted.
3. Children sang the National Anthem.
4. The Flag was saluted, and patriotic songs were sung.
5. The Schoolmaster gave a history of the Flag.
6. Readings and recitations illustrating heroic duty and self sacrifice for the Nation.
7. National Anthem sung, the Flag saluted, and children dismissed.

Edward Holmes, later to be Chief Inspector of Elementary Schools, had written in 1899 of the village school as having a national imperial role:

> "Its business is to turn out youthful citizens rather than hedgers and ditchers ..... Preparing children for the battle of life (a battle which will ... be fought in all parts of the British Empire)." *(Report of the Board of Education for 1899 - 1900, pp 1900, Vol XIX, pp 254-6; - cited in Pamela Horn: The Victorian and Edwardian Schoolchild, 2010, p.53).*

Young men had tried to enlist in the Army when the Boer War had begun, but the health and physique of many was so poor that large numbers were turned down as recruits. The British Government was becoming more and more pre-occupied with the security of an ever-expanding Empire. Recruits were constantly needed not only for the physical defence of the nation or its colonies by the Army and the Navy, but also for an expanding Colonial Service. Such service took young men, and sometimes their young families as well, to 'unhealthy climes'. A sense of patriotism and a healthy nation were required.

The foundation of personal good health was essential for the survival of those who would staff the Empire. The health and well being of the children of the mother country was now seen to be an important necessity. The State responded by empowering the newly established Local Education Authorities. It allowed them to set in hand the provision of school meals and the medical monitoring of children through a School Medical Service, which was given the power to give free medical treatment to young people a few years later (preceding the National Health Service by almost forty years). It has to be said that about half of the LEA's did not respond with alacrity.

School medical inspections began in 1907, but in the early years whilst many diagnoses were made requiring treatment, in some districts only a quarter of the children ended up being treated because of a shortage of funds, as well as the shortage of medical resources. From a later period, one Darsham ex-pupil had vivid recollections of being checked for nits: "The nit nurse used to go through every child's hair with the same pencil - and without cleaning it." In 1913, the Chief

Medical Officer estimated that out of six million elementary school children in England and Wales, half had decayed teeth, a tenth had a serious vision defect, and another tenth were unclean in their bodies' (i.e. covering everything from being unwashed to being verminous). At Darsham School in October 1914, a boy was slippered after being sent home twice for a change of linen.

A "Model Course of Physical Training" had been issued by the Board of Education in London in 1902. It was largely based on Army training methods. It was assimilated into the curriculum at Darsham School fairly rapidly, and provoked two occasions (otherwise almost unknown during this period), when the cane was used. In May 1907 and again in May 1914, boys were caned "for inattention at Drill." At the end of 1908, the School Log Book records that there was a visit from the Physical Education Inspector of the East Suffolk County Council, a post reflecting the national importance being attached to physical development.

With the outbreak of war in August 1914, the disruption to family life through fathers joining the Armed Forces was immediate. Children's school life was soon disrupted by discipline problems following the start of the new school year in September, and in some ways children were among the earliest groups of the population to suffer from the many psychological effects of war. During the course of the First World War seventy-five men from all sections of village society in Darsham served in the Armed Forces and so a large proportion of the local families were affected. Many of these young men were former pupils of Darsham School, including Harold Aldrich who joined the Suffolk Regiment, Special Reserve, shortly after the outbreak of war. As 2nd Lieutenant Harold Andrew Aldrich, he was awarded the Military Cross for conspicuous gallantry whilst under fire, after serving three years in the trenches. Sadly sixteen other Darsham men died during the conflict.

While fathers went off to war, mothers were encouraged to go out to work. Meantime, youngsters could be expected to stay away from school to look after younger siblings. Locally there was no School Attendance Officer to act in the interests of schooling, since the person in post, Sergeant Major Peaty, was noted as being interned in Holland, presumably having been recalled to his regiment. In fact nationally, expectations of enforcing school attendance were relaxed, which was widely interpreted on farms as meaning the children should work on the land again rather than go to school.

Disruption to schooling was inevitable and seemingly endless. In the middle of all of this disruption to the normal pattern of schooling in the village, the admission of three Canadian children to the school is recorded in the Log Book. They and their mother were staying at the Fox public house in Darsham. The children's names were Victor, Beatrice and Edward Hart. The family were probably relatives of the Licensee, Mr Alfred Hart. After three weeks they moved on to Ipswich. What impression did they make on the children of

Darsham? Why were they in Darsham? What happened to them as war progressed? — perhaps symbolic of the turmoil of the times — nothing is recorded.

Between 1915 and 1916, there was a significant increase in the number of punishments recorded in the Punishment Book. There must have been a vacuum in domestic discipline with family life disrupted by the absence of male family members away at war, as well as mothers working away from the home. Roles became uncertain, and children would not know what kind of role they were expected to play. There would have been frayed nerves, grief and anger, and these complex emotions would make themselves felt in school, as home life became suddenly more difficult. Amidst all of this anxiety one nine year old had a classic dose of naughtiness. In October 1916, William Knights, the son of Robert Knights, a farm labourer at Gravel Pit Farm, Darsham received two strokes of the cane across his fingers for daubing a stile in Low Road with Cherry Blossom boot polish. There must have been interesting consequences for the unsuspecting users of the stile! And worse, Master Knights and four other Darsham boys were punished for interfering with roadmen's tools — four strokes across the fingers administered with a ruler for each child; some kids always want to stray beyond the bounds of common decency!

During the war years there were shortages of food and other supplies, children's health was affected, and bad weather tended to play havoc with attendance over and above the circumstances already mentioned. None-the-less Mr Ludbrook, maintaining excellent relationships with the village, helping to support and stabilise attendance figures. He was probably highly respected by many of the children's parents because he would have taught many of those people himself.

However, in order to help the war effort, the school year was shortened in 1917 from four hundred sessions to three hundred and twenty sessions (registers are marked twice each day), so that there was more holiday time available for children to join in the national effort.

In Darsham, as part of the war effort, two local children's organisations were formed that may well have been unique. In late 1914 or early 1915, the girls were formed into 'Busy Bees', and were under the direction of the Queen Bee, Miss Constable, who was the live-in housekeeper for the Thornhill family at Darsham Cottage. Later, at the beginning of 1917, the 'Order (or Guild) of Active Ants' was inaugurated as a companion order for the boys, under the guidance of Master Ant, Revd Dr. Tennant. Both groups were dissolved once the war was over at the end of 1918.

The 'Busy Bees' were; Laura Crisp; Faith Flegg; Alice Fuller; Mabel Glanfield; Elsie Hacon; Adeline Hambling; Dorothy Hambling; Alice Martin; Kitty Martin; Doris Mower; Hilda Spicer and Kate Taylor. Hilda Spicer was a pupil teacher at the school. (There is a photograph of the 'Busy Bees' in this

Darsham 'Busy Bees' 1914 - 1918.

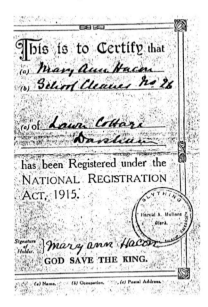

School Cleaner's Certificate, 1915.

MILITARY CROSS FOR GALLANTRY.

2nd-Lieut. H. A. ALDRICH.

A supplement to the "London Gazette" announces that the King has been pleased to approve of the award of the Military Cross to a number of officers, amongst whom appears the name of Second-Lieut Harold Andrew Aldrich, Suffolk Regt., Special Reserve, second son of Mr. A. H. Aldrich, of Brampton Old Hall, who gained this honour for conspicuous gallantry and devotion to duty. Although his platoon was inflilade by heavy machine gun fire and bombed in front, he maintained his position with great gallantry until forced to withdraw. On the following day his position was again subjected to very heavy machine-gun fire, and his platoon suffered serious casualties. Throughout this period he moved about fearlessly under heavy fire, affording his men a most inspiring example of coolness and determination. Second-Lieut. Aldrich joined H.M. Forces in October, 1914, and was attached to the 4th Suffolks. He has been in France for three years.

We are pleased to note that Capt H. A. Aldrich of Bramfield has recently been the recipient from the War Office of the Military Cross, awarded by His Majesty the King in recognition of the valuable services rendered by him during the War.

Press Report re Gallantry Award to Harold Andrew Aldrich, former pupil at Darsham School.

book but, unfortunately, the girls cannot be individually identified). The idea was to work to produce things that might be of use to members of the Armed Forces, including Darsham men, who were fighting in the war.

The Busy Bees met every Saturday at Darsham Cottage, the home of Mrs Thornhill. This would be a sewing class to help the Red Cross. Mrs Thornhill provided eighty yards of material at the beginning of 1915. In three months, the girls had made a hundred and fifty-one bandages. Each Busy Bee was given a penny with which to trade, and after three months a total of £1. 14s. 10d. had been raised for the purchase of more materials for the sewing class. Their next aim was to send a parcel to each of the twenty-four men of Darsham then fighting for 'King & Country'. By the end of the year the girls had collected enough wool to make twenty-four pairs of mittens. There were twenty-two scarves from the wool of an anonymous donor, one scarf from Mrs Spicer and one scarf from Miss Spicer. £1.10s came "from a smoker"; £2. 5s. 10d. from the sale of two baskets of wool; 12lbs of plum puddings came from Mrs Thornhill and five shillings towards postage. The girls were able to send a parcel to each Darsham Serviceman that contained:

1 Scarf   *½ lb. Plum Pudding*
1 Pair Mittens   *½ lb. Raisins*
1 Pair Socks   *1 Tin Condensed*
                       Milk
1 Pair Bootlaces   *Notepaper & Cards*

1 Handkerchief   1 Pencil
1 Packet Spearmint   1 Box Matches
Six Cigars

In 1916, the Bees' organised a sale of work which realised the sum of £16. 18s. 6d. to buy further material for their Red Cross work. In April, they collected and sent an Easter gift of 200 eggs to Halesworth Hospital and during the summer holiday, they collected and sent another batch of 200 eggs, again to Halesworth Hospital where wounded servicemen were being nursed. In September, the Busy Bees organised a sale of work and a garden fete at the Vicarage and raised the sum of £46. 6s. 6d, which was devoted to sending a Christmas parcel to each of the sixty-five Darsham men then serving. In the October of this busy year, the girls sent another consignment of one hundred useful articles to the W.H.S. Depot at Ipswich and as a last effort for the year; they collected the sum of £2. 9s. 6d. to make forty pairs of gloves 'for our brave mine-sweepers.'

By 1917, most of the girls had left the village, but those who remained sent a large parcel of useful garments to the Ipswich Depot of the Red Cross and again sent a parcel of 200 eggs to Halesworth Hospital.

Members of the 'Active Ants' were:- Rupert Balls; George Denny; Chester Flegg; Freddie Flegg; Wilfred Holmes; Alec Noller; Valentine Noller; Robert Norman; Harvey Smith; and Jack Taylor. They pledged themselves, under certain rules and conditions, to be of use in any capacity according to their powers - to run errands and do other odd jobs in house or parish, in fact to be the little handymen of the parish. For each service they expected some small payment and each had a box for that purpose. The object was that the boys as well as the girls should "do their bit" during the war years. The box contents were devoted to a War Fund chosen by the boys. The total sum for 1917, their first year, amounted to £5. 3s. 10d. and this was given to Ipswich Hospital for wounded soldiers. At the end of 1918, the "Master Ant", Dr. Tennant, reported that with several boxes not yet handed in, the collection that year amounted to £1. 14s. 1d., which was donated to a charity for sailors.

The object of these children's organisations was for the girls and boys to do their bit for the war effort. Perhaps the girls were quicker off the mark. They may have been of a different age group, or it could have been that the boys were having to spend more time helping on the land. The outcomes are plain enough. There would have been pride generated in what they were achieving; their self-confidence and sense of community would be built up in the process, and perhaps even the awful fear of the unknowns of the times might have been diminished for these children to a degree by having something tangible to aim at. It is likely that similarities with the Scouting and Guiding movements are genuine; these organisations would have been well known, having been founded in 1907. The existence of the collection boxes given to the Active Ants seems closely linked with the ideas of 'Bob a Job' but which was the forerunner?

In 1917 and 1918, the Board of Education in London, in co-operation with the Food Production Department of the War Office, launched a national Blackberry Scheme in which Suffolk children took part. Huge quantities of blackberries were gathered and sent to a jam factory at Ipswich where they were made into jam for the troops.

Children also had to gather conkers (horse-chestnuts). One of the solvents required in making cordite is acetone, which can be extracted from conkers. A factory in Kings Lynn was converted for the extraction process, and conkers were gathered by children all over the country and delivered to railway stations. However, in spite of managing to cope with 3,000 tons of conkers, the factory became overwhelmed with horse chestnuts, so many consignments never reached their destination. No shortage of cordite appears to have been the consequence; over a quarter of a billion shells were used by the British Army and Royal Navy during the conflict.

Continuing effects of the war were not generally recorded in Darsham School Log Book, other than the fates of ex-pupils on active service. However two incidents were mentioned for June 1917. There was an air raid warning which was given but proved to be a false alarm. The other incident recorded was the bombing raid on Suffolk on the night of 16/17th June. This was the most important local attack of the whole war. Aeroplane B401 brought down Zeppelin L48 over Theberton with great loss of life. B401 was the first aeroplane made by Ransome Sims & Jefferies Ltd., the major British manufacturer of agricultural machinery, based in Ipswich, when the firm was put on a war footing to construct aircraft.

Though there is little mention of the war in the school Log Book, the subject most certainly came up in their lessons. The exercise book of Margery Esther Alexander, running from 1913 to 1918, contains arithmetic exercises and essays, which were called compositions in those days. In 1914 she composed an essay on 'What is a loaf of bread?'. However, in 1915, she writes 'A Letter to a Soldier at the Front' and 'A Letter to a Friend' in which she refers to an uncle about to go to the Front and two cousins already there.

In 1916, she describes the life of a Red Cross Nurse at the Front as dangerous whether in France, Serbia or Egypt. In 1917, she describes submarine warfare, explaining how our submarines sink only enemy warships and merchant ships but that German submarines also sink Hospital Ships and Liners. This composition also has a hand drawn illustration showing the head of a man peering through a periscope. In 1918, an essay was about the Home Front, on how to economise with food and clothing. All these compositions received the mark V.G., 9/10' the composition on the submarine gaining 9½/10, keen approval from the teacher. Even one of the sums set had a topical theme asking, "Find the Simple Interest of £75 War Loan for 10 years at 5% per annum." Margery gave the correct answer.

In 1918, Spanish 'flu arrived, and the school was closed when the Armistice came. It was closed for significant periods until March 1919 because of the epidemic. On 18th and 19th July, 1919, a holiday was given for the 'Peace Celebrations.' Published in the Leiston Observer and the Halesworth Times are reports relating to Darsham:

"**PEACE CELEBRATIONS**: By kind permission of Mr J. W. Parry- Crooke. the celebrations were held in the grounds of Darsham House. Small committees assisted by willing workers, carried out the programme to every bodies satisfaction. A bounteous tea was provided for all.
If absent from infirmity or other cause, a parcel was sent to the absent one. Just before leaving, the children received bananas, oranges and chocolates. A show of fruit and vegetables was held. This was well supported. Prizes to the value of about £8 were distributed. The fruit was sold to Mr Scott Catchpole and the vegetables were sent to the East Suffolk & Ipswich Hospital. Sports for juveniles and for adults were arranged by Capt. C. Parry-Crooke and Mr A.K. Mann. They were assisted by Mr Stokes and Mr Geater and a lengthy programme was carried through, no less than £15 being distributed amongst the winners. There were also guessing competitions for two black pigs, given by Messrs. Scott and Raymond Catchpole. One of the pigs was secured by Mrs Banstead and the other by Mr A.H. Smith (High Street). There was also a hoop-la under the chestnuts. This contained toys galore, given by Mrs Parry-Crooke. It was in the charge of the maids of Darsham House and was well

Name in full *Margery Esther Alexander* Age *12 years*
School *Darsham Council*
Last Term in Standard VI., Date *30th March 1917*

COMPOSITION: To consist of—(1) An easy Essay; (2) A Letter on a selected subject; (3) The reproduction of a story read; (4) The description of the subject of a picture supplied; (5) The filling up of a story given in outline; (6) or a description of Historical, Geographical or Scientific subjects studied during the year.

Submarine Warfare.

Submarines are boats which can go along under the water, with only the periscope, which is a hollow tube, shaped like a printed L turned upside down, showing a little way out of the water. The submarines are cigar shaped, and have, beside the periscope, a conning-tower, which is round.

The submarines are used to torpedo enemy ships, and our submarines sink German merchant ships, but not hospital ships, or liners. The German submarines, however, do sink liners and hospital ships. Just recently, they torpedoed a ship which was bringing home wounded soldiers, and they even fire on the people whilst they are in the sea, which is a cruel thing to do.

The submarines, I think, are used in war-time to sink the enemy's warships, troop-

Essay by Margery Esther Alexander

Name in full *Margery Esther Alexander*   Age *12 yrs*
School *Darsham Council*
Last Term in Standard VI., Date *30th March 1917*

ARITHMETIC.

No. 1. How often is 195yds 1ft 8ins. contained in 1 mile?

```
3 1760 yds in 1 mile
    36
  10560
   5280
  63360 ins
```

```
  195 yds 1ft 8ins
       3
     586
      12
    7040 ins
```

7040) 63360
       9 times

No. 3. Reduce $\frac{19}{31}$ of 2/7 to the decimal of 15/10

$\frac{19}{31}$ of 2/7 = $\frac{5}{7}$ ·· $\frac{d}{7}$

$\frac{x \cdot x}{\cancel{x5} \cdot \cancel{x6}} \cdot \frac{1}{10} = \cdot 1$ Ans
$\frac{1}{10}$

No. 6. A ship has provision for 320 men for 91 days. How long would they last 13 men?

men   men   days
As 13 : 320 :: 91 : x

7 × 320 = 2240 days

Ans 2240 days

patronised by the children. On leaving the grounds, many adjourned to the Priory to witness a display of fireworks given by Mr Scott Catchpole. The soldiers and sailors, demobbed and still serving, to the number of 35 were entertained to dinner by Mr and Mrs Parry-Crooke in the billiard room of Darsham House, which was gaily bedecked with flags. A hearty greeting was extended to all those present and appreciation of Mr and Mrs Parry-Crooke's kindness was concurred by all when Lt. Ludbrook proposed the health of that gentleman and his family."

On 6th November, 1919 national newspapers published "The King's Letter to his People", which read as follows:-

First Anniversary of Armistice Day.
"To ALL MY PEOPLE, Tuesday next, 11th November, is the first anniversary of the Armistice, which stayed the world-wide carnage of the four preceding years and marked the victory of right and freedom. I believe that my people in every part of the Empire fervently wish to perpetuate the memory of that great deliverance, and of those who laid down their lives to achieve it. To afford an opportunity for the universal expression of this feeling, it is my desire and hope that at the hour when the Armistice came into force, the eleventh hour of the eleventh day of the eleventh month, there may be, for the brief space of two minutes, a complete suspension of all our normal activities. During that time except in the rare cases where this may be impractical, all work, all sound, and all locomotion should cease, so that in

perfect stillness, the thoughts of everyone may be concentrated on reverent remembrance of the glorious dead. No elaborate organisation appears to be necessary. At a given signal, which can easily be arranged to suit the circumstances of each locality, I believe that we shall all gladly interrupt our business and pleasure, whatever it may be, and unite in this simple service of silence and remembrance."

On 11th November, **'The King's Letter to his People'** was read to the pupils of Darsham School, and a two minute silence observed from 11 o'clock.

The world changed as a result of the First World War, and Darsham did not escape the changes. One major effect on village life was changes caused by the long-term decline in the number of children in the parish. In 1914, there had been eighty-nine children on the register, but by 1932, the numbers had dwindled to thirty-two. The Methodist Chapel was able to maintain a Sunday school throughout this period but the 1st Darsham Boy Scouts formed in 1921 only had a short existence. The 1st Darsham Girl Guides formed a year earlier in 1920 lasted until 1932.

The Old Comrades Association for returning servicemen began to hold events for Darsham school children in 1922. They had accepted the offer of a surplus wooden hut from the War Department. It was built as a clubroom for their association, and still stands today, now as the Village Hall. On January 11th 1922, the Halesworth Times reported:

"**SCHOOL TREAT**. The ex- Servicemen of Darsham on January 2nd., provided a most enjoyable afternoon in their hut for the school children of the parish and other children attending the school. The proceedings began with an excellent tea presided over by willing lady helpers after which games and several bran tubs, filled to the brim with gifts all given by the ex-Servicemen, brought much amusement and merriment. Mrs Parry-Crooke, on behalf of the children, cordially thanked the ex- Servicemen for their kindness in arranging the treat."

This occasion must have stirred memories of the parcels sent by the Darsham children during the war years. The treat became a delightful annual event.

The winds of change were set to blow harder. As well as massive public debt following the war, the economy had fallen into depression. It was argued that public spending had to be cut. In Darsham the effect was to precipitate the resignation of Mr Ludbrook as headmaster. He had held the post since 1893, with continuing success for the school. He had also been thoroughly involved in local affairs, first as a Parish Councillor between 1902 and 1910, a position which he would hold again from 1940 until 1944. In the meantime he had been Parish Clerk between 1911 and 1920.

Chapter Six

**Making the Best of Things
1925 - 1945.**

From the Halesworth Times, 25th November, 1925:

"**PRESENTATION**: A large and representative gathering of villagers of Darsham assembled in the Comrades Hut, for the purpose of showing their esteem and respect to MR & MRS G.F.C. LUDBROOK, who on medical advice have retired from their position as Schoolmaster and Schoolmistress, which they have occupied with marked success for nearly thirty two years.

Mr. A.K. Mann, Chairman of the School Managers, who was supported by Mr J.W. Parry-Crooke, the Rev. Dr. C. Tennant M.A. (Vicar) and Capt. R.J. Catchpole, remarked that he and others had felt that such a long period of successful work and the help ungrudgingly given in parochial matters by Mr and Mrs Ludbrook, should not be allowed to pass without tangible recognition. He had therefore invited subscriptions from present and past residents and there had been a ready and generous response.

Mr Parry-Crooke said that he had the letter which Mr Ludbrook wrote to his late father, who was then Chairman of the School Board, accepting the appointment. Of those who were then Managers, only two remained, Mr R. Lovett and Mr F.W. Brooke, the well known artist. During his long career, the work of the school had been maintained at a high level and many commendatory official reports had been received. As for Mrs Ludbrook, she was regarded not only as a teacher but also as a Mother to those under her charge. The speakers referred to Mr Ludbrook's many activities including those of the organisation of fetes for the British Red Cross and the East Suffolk and Ipswich Hospital and said that his life must have been an extremely busy one. Dr Tennant and Capt. Catchpole re-echoed the sentiments of the previous speakers.

Mr Mann then formally made the presentations. They consisted of a solid mahogany bookcase to Mr Ludbrook and to Mrs Ludbrook a solid mahogany bureau, inlaid with rosewood, both articles being in the Queen Anne style Affixed were suitable inscriptions and a blotter in crocodile leather was another gift.

The school children had already given Mrs Ludbrook a flower bowl and Mr and Mrs Parry-Crooke had made a personal presentation of a pair of massive cut glass silver rimmed flower vases. The school children had also made a present of a pipe to their old Master.

Mr Ludbrook thanked the speakers and the subscribers on behalf of his wife and himself and said that the gifts would act as a constant reminder of the happy relationship that had existed between themselves and the parishioners for the past thirty-two years. They were still remaining among them and would always be pleased to do anything in his power for the village he loved so well."

In this retirement tribute, mention is made of Mr and Mrs Ludbrook's ungrudging help, given not only in their professional capacity as teachers, but also in parochial matters. There is particular reference to Mr Ludbrook organising fetes for the Red Cross and the East Suffolk & Ipswich Hospital. This is not the picture of a person wishing to retire from a position of leadership in the community, and indeed he continued to be involved in parish affairs as was mentioned at the end of the last chapter. The Halesworth Times states that the Ludbrooks retired 'as a result of medical advice'. The paper was obviously not given access to exchanges between the East Suffolk Education Authority and the school managers, and between the school managers and the Ludbrooks.

The county authority had advised the school managers that they were looking to cut costs by appointing a headmistress to Darsham School. It wasn't until 1961 that women teachers achieved equal pay, and so a headmistress for Darsham School in 1925 would come cheaper. The school managers approached Mr Ludbrook to see if he would accept a reduction in pay. Mr Ludbrook, aged fifty-eight, decided to retire, having been in charge of the school since 1893, and a headmistress was duly appointed. Another period followed in which appointments to the school did not last long.

The Ludbrooks lived on in their cottage in The Street, the cottage now known as 'Bumble Bee Cottage'. Mr Ludbrook lived until shortly before the end of the war in 1945.

Darsham School was not likely to attract a teacher with significant professional ambitions. Numbers on the roll were destined to fall off, and the school would already have been designated as having to lose a teacher, becoming a two-teacher establishment. It would not have been difficult to find out that a male head teacher had retired in 1925 rather than accept a lower salary. A woman would be taking on the same amount of work, as well as facing re-organisation, for a lower salary. Although Mr Ludbrook would have tried not to cause difficulties for the new appointee, the teacher would have been very aware that this successful and popular retired head teacher was living just down the road.

None the less Miss Elsie Harper took up an appointment as Head Teacher in 1933. She married in that year, becoming Mrs Quadling. She joined an infant teacher, Miss Ellen Ashwell, who had taken up her post in 1927, and who remained at the school until 1943. Mrs Quadling remained as head teacher until her death in 1954. These two ladies, of very different temperaments, worked together and provided the backbone of the school for difficult years of depression and the war.

This was a very different time in which to be a teacher, even more so to be a head teacher in a small rural school like

Darsham. Educational debate was vigorous, though often not much to the point when it had to be translated into action at the local level, nor was there likely to be sufficient funding, let alone training or advice about how to do the job properly. It must have seemed that generally the expectation was that more would have to done with less.

The wartime arguments about the extent to which children should be involved in the war effort, whether they should be 'earners' or 'learners' gave ground to questions of child welfare in the inter-war period. The broad canvas of this argument concerned the extent to which State responsibility, in other words the education system, could be allowed to erode parental responsibility.

As part of this debate there were also concerns about how far poverty and poor maternal practices could be the cause of poor child health. There was a nutritional aspect to unravel as well. Who should be responsible for children's food during the school day? Would a meal provided by the State (of course organised by the two teachers for the forty-five or so children at Darsham at lunch-time), diminish a mother's sense of responsibility; or reversing the question, shouldn't taking children into a State-run facility during the day imply a responsibility to feed them during that time? Set against the poverty of many families during this time of severe depression, would not feeding children mean that they would be too hungry to learn?

There was also the influence of the Children and Young Persons Act of 1933. The presumption was that young people who offended were psychologically disturbed as a result of having suffered poor social and physical environments. Both those children being classed as neglected, and the children categorised as delinquent were regarded as being in need of care and protection. However, some thought that physical punishment, i.e. birching, had real value. A member of the House of Lords was recorded in debate as describing the desire for the abolition of whipping as, "this effeminate, over-humanitarian, ultra-sentimental view". *(Cited in Mayall & V. Morrow: "You can help your country: English children's work during the Second World War", 2011, p.54).*

However, in spite of the Act, in the light of a continued rise in juvenile crime in the 1930's, young delinquents continued to receive harsh treatment, including hard work, tough living conditions, poor diet and physical punishment whilst in detention. Pastoral advice through intervention from the Church, which already felt that its views were being ignored, seems to have been sidelined; the Church Times had earlier recorded the comment: "The increase of crime among juveniles is almost entirely due to the cessation of definite religious instruction in the Schools". *(Church Times, 14th September, 1923).* As a result, in the sphere of education there remained mixed messages about the value of physical punishment versus special education. It was never made clear about which was to be the direction in which education should move.

The tension between the carrot and the stick, as a means of correcting behaviour, continued to be unresolved in the midst of an era of huge social change. It is then perhaps not surprising to learn that Mrs Quadling always found the practice of discipline problematic. That same tension between stick and carrot could well be used to suggest, even encapsulate, the symptoms of her obviously complex, but striking character. She erred on the side of severity in the hope that this would lead to her children becoming members of a responsible adult society.

A case involving three Darsham boys, which came up before the Juvenile Court at Halesworth is pertinent in demonstrating Mrs Quadling's way of thinking. Presumably it was at her instigation that the matter was referred to the police, but she was prepared to provide evidence as to at least one of the boys' previous good characters when the matter came before the Court. In September 1937, Harry Tovell, William Pooley and Dennis Flegg stood accused of malicious damage to Darsham School garden. Mrs Quadling appeared as a witness and gave evidence concerning the boys' family circumstances and their behaviour while they had been pupils at the school in earlier years. Miss Ashwell also gave evidence.

What happened was reported in the Halesworth Times of 8th September 1937:

"On 22nd July at 8.30.pm., the Darsham School teacher, Miss Ashwell had seen two Darsham youths, aged sixteen years and a third aged fifteen years, riding their bicycles around the front playground of Darsham School. They had then disappeared into the back playground. Ten minutes later they reappeared at the front of the school, cycling round and round in the road and throwing pea pods at each other. The following day, Mrs Quadling made an inspection of the school gardens at the rear of the school and found that stakes marking plots had been pulled up, bicycle marks were all around the front garden and eight rows of peas had been stripped."

Two of the boys appeared in Court with their parents. The third boy failed to appear and a warrant was issued for his appearance a week later. Pc Keable of Yoxford gave evidence of interviewing the boys. One fifteen year old admitted going onto the gardens and the sixteen year old admitted picking pea pods. Mrs Quadling gave evidence that one of the boys had no father and was the eldest of a large family. At school he had been very well behaved but during the last few months had got very much out of hand. The two boys were **"placed on probation for two years, would have to be in bed by 9.0.pm., in the summer and 8.0.pm in the winter. Furthermore, they were not to go to a cinema for** three months".

In the press report, the boy who had failed to appear in Court was referred to as "A ringleader of a local gang." When the boy eventually appeared at the second hearing, he received the same punishment as his co-offenders. The Vicar, the Rev. Maitland, appeared at the Court to inform the Magistrates that "There is no gang in Darsham in the sense that the word was applied to groups of boys in newspaper reports".

Life in general was still fairly Spartan for village families in those days. Peggy Irene Boreham was at Darsham School from 1932 to 1937. Until she could ride a bicycle herself, she was taken on her mother's bike, on the carrier, to school and back all the way from the High Street, Darsham. Other memories of journeys to school on winter mornings are equally vivid. An ex-pupil remembers cycling all the way up to the Street from her home near the station, and then cycling down the Street to the school, leaving her bicycle at Orion Cottage, near the school, ready for the return journey. She recalls Horlicks or cocoa on arrival at school on cold mornings, the powder and milk being provided by Mrs Parry-Crooke of Darsham House. Another pupil remembers the cocoa and Horlicks as being, "rather watery but warming." Later, when a third of a pint of free milk was provided for each child, the crate would be stood by the stove in cold weather "to take the chill off". It is related that on wet days, coats were hung round the fireguard in the large schoolroom.

Darsham Pupils - 1928
(Teachers - Miss Ashwell & Miss Lamb)

Back Row - left to right
Mary Alexander; Joan Alexander; Albert Norman; Ernest Alexander; Stanford Goddard; Bill Watling; Bert Sharpe; Arthur Green; Dick Watling; Florence Green.

Middle Row - left to right
Evelyn Alexander; Stanley Alexander; Alice Norman; Cyril Green; Molly Green; Joyce Fuller; Elsie Goodchild; Hilda Flegg; ..?.. Rose Flegg; Vera Ellis.

Front Row - left to right
Arthur Alexander; Harry Watling; Lennie Goodchild; Bill Brabben; Doug Sharpe; Ken Smith; Ted Green; Toddy Fuller.

Darsham Pupils - 1931/32

Back Row - left to right
Arthur Alexander; Kenneth Smith; Gladys Rouse; Ted Green; Flo Gooch; Lennie Goodchild; Molly Green; William Brabben & Edwin Robinson

Middle Row - left to right
Vera Seaman; Lorna Tovell; Joyce Fuller; Vera? Barker Norah Cook; Evelyn Alexander; Hazel Smith; Hilda Flegg; Renee Walker; Joan Barker; Elsie Goodchild.

Front Row - left to right
Terry Walker; Dennis Flegg; Bill Robinson; Harry Cooper; George Robinson; Stanley Alexander: Henry Tovell & Harry Martin.

Water had to be collected in a bucket from the pump opposite the school, and two enamel mugs were tied to it should anyone require a drink; the comment 'also used for hand washing when necessary' perhaps needs some clarification! There was a distinct lack of concern for health and safety issues compared to modern times.

In spite of the fact that Januaries were piercingly cold, Februaries characterised by snow and/or fog, and March by the 'flu, the school's games teams had emerged as worthy competitors against other schools. In 1928, during the interregnum between Mr Ludbrook and Mrs Quadling, the Darsham School Football Team had defeated Theberton 3 - 0, and the Darsham School Girls Netball Team had beaten Westleton 6 - 1. Albeit in 1930 the Drill Instructor complained that the playground was unfit for drill.

The continuing presence of drill in the curriculum implies that children were still being prepared for the possibility of military service. Similarly, patriotic idealism remained as aspiration; linked to a sense of personal fulfilment, witness the life of King Arthur as an example:

> "The great men of the land came eager to draw the sword from the stone. Each tried in turn but with all their strength none could pull it out. Last of all came a boy named Arthur; he laid his hand on the hilt, and in a moment out came the sword." *(A Transcript Exercise*

from the exercise book of Kenneth Smith, Darsham C. School, Std.2, circa 1928, when he was aged eight years).

Kenneth Smith was the son of Sydney & Priscilla Smith of Brussels Green, and this is from his 'progress book', which still survives.

So, the Spartan ideal continued to permeate Darsham School life throughout much of the 1930's. In a survey of elementary school buildings in 1935 - 1936, it was observed that eighty per cent of the buildings were not fit for purpose. At Darsham School on 20th December 1937, the temperature in the classroom at 10.00am., was 34°F (1°C), and two days later the school was closed at 11.00.am., as it was 'so very cold.' The ink had frozen in the inkwells all week.

However, there were innovations within the curriculum, and other new practices, including the opportunities for taking children further afield for outside events, as transport became more readily available. At the same time the situation regarding falling numbers of pupils had to be dealt with. With only sixty pupils on the roll, Mrs Quadling made the first change in 1935. The eighteen senior pupils were the largest class, but they would fit into the smaller classroom at the back of the school, where they were taught by Mrs Quadling. The forty-two juniors and infants were put in the larger front classroom, the two classes being separated by a curtain. By 1937 there were now only forty-seven children at

Darsham Pupils - 1933/34

Back Row - left to right
Stephen Saker; Pamela Barker; Joan Burrows; Ronald London; Dorothy London; Geoffrey London; Betty Knights; May Fairs; Dilly Sharpe.

Middle Row - left to right
Betty Alexander; Nancy Robinson; Joyce London; Robert Grimwood; Ethel Thurston; Sheila Tovell; Sheila Saker; Marjorie London; Peggy Boreham; Winnie Saker.

Front Row - left to right
Cyril? Smith; Harry Tovell; .....?; Cyril Green; Frank (Plummy) Cook; Gordon Goddard.

Darsham Pupils - 1935

Darsham Pupils - 1947

the school. East Suffolk declared the school to be a two-teacher school. Because there were now very few infants, Miss Ashwell took the infants and Standard 1 together into the smaller classroom, and Mrs Quadling had all the older children in the large room.

As to innovations, the first record of an "Open Day" for parents and managers comes from the time before Mrs Quadling was appointed. On 10th November, 1930 the School Log Book carries the first record of this important event, which over the years since has done much to break down the mystique of what goes on in schools, and has helped to bring much closer relations between staff and parents in furthering pupils' educational development. Then there were those days out; there were holidays for the Yoxford Fete and the Halesworth Flower Show and Sports. There were also the annual holidays for the Sunday School outings, and in 1931, there was an outing by train (and trolley bus) to visit the Engineering Works of Ransome & Rapier at Ipswich.

Peggy Boreham remembers both boys and girls having to learn to knit. She sat by Wilfred "Dilly" Sharp and Derek Lugo who were both very good at dropping stitches in their knitting, getting her to pick up the stitch and "knit to the end of the row for them." Evelyn Evans (Evelyn Alexander as she was when a pupil at Darsham School between 1925 and 1933), remembers that from the age of eleven, the girls walked to Yoxford School on Fridays where they were instructed in laundering during the summer and cooking in the winter. Some of the laundry must have belonged to the teachers because on one occasion Evelyn inadvertently ruined an item of a teacher's underwear whilst ironing it. She was not asked to do ironing again! Flat irons, of course, were heated on metal contraptions that hung around the stove; no electric irons in those days. The boys attended at Yoxford school on Tuesdays, for woodwork lessons. Evelyn also remembers that in 1927 she and other pupils formed the Guard of Honour at the wedding of her first teacher, Miss Kathleen Stokes, who was married at Darsham Church, next to the school.

Sports replaced drill. There had been sporting competitions at the Halesworth Flower Show & Sports, probably at least partly for men, but on 29th May, 1935, Darsham School was closed for the area sports at Reydon. On that occasion George Robinson, aged 13 years, of Hill Farm, Lymballs Lane, Darsham, won the 200 yards. Though George would work on the land for most of his life, when there was no farm work in the late 1930's he went fishing out of Lowestoft. The result was that when he joined the Royal Navy for World War II, he was seen as an ideal candidate to serve on minesweepers out of Lowestoft. Not an enviable job!

The school garden was an innovation which may have aroused mixed feelings among the pupils. Garden produce earned first prize for the Halesworth Flower Show & Sports in

1931 and 1932. On 6th June, 1935 teachers took twelve children to the Suffolk Show at Halesworth. There was a discussion about the school garden being too large for the number of boys left to cultivate it. Was it a memory of the extra effort extracted from those boys which prompted a revenge attack in 1937 ending in that Court case? At any rate, any misgivings that children may have had about digging would have been set aside when the garden was put into full production at the beginning of the war.

The introduction of a wireless set in October 1937, obtained from the proceeds of jumble sales and concerts, was probably a more popular innovation with the children. School broadcasts could now be included as part of lessons. The first wireless talk that Darsham children listened to at school was a history play about Greeks and Persians. The sounds of the Battle of Thermopylae would have seemed miraculous in comparison with copying diagrams from the school blackboard. Sadly, the reality of the preparation for war was about to arrive in Darsham School. The following year the children, with the exception of one mother who refused permission, had to bring their gas masks to school to be fitted.

There were other lighter moments during 1937, the year in which the inkwells froze. On 11th. May, there was a holiday to celebrate the Coronation of King George VI and Queen Elizabeth. Each Darsham school child was presented with a silver plated teaspoon to commemorate the event. On the top of the spoons, the heads of their Majesties were displayed, on the bowl, "crowned 1937", and on the reverse "Darsham School", were stamped. Sixty-six years later the authors were shown one of these spoons, in mint condition, having obviously been cherished by the recipient.

It was in 1937 that the first pupil from Darsham School won a scholarship to the grammar school at Beccles. Peggy Boreham has said that, "With some reluctance I left Darsham School in July 1937, having been the first child from there to sit the exam and win a scholarship. No direct transport in those days, I had to catch the 7.40.am., train to Beccles, half an hour on the train and then a two mile walk to Sir John Leman School where I spent the rest of my school days, mostly war years. But my happiest days were at Darsham." Two years later, in July 1939, two more pupils won scholarships to Sir John Leman School. Barbara Lanham and Dorothy Nunn both began the daily train journeys to Beccles in the September.

At the beginning of 1939, there was a school treat. In early January, the whole of Darsham School went by bus to Norwich to the pantomime. The Halesworth Times of 12th January, 1939 gives a fulsome report:

> "The children of Darsham Primary School had a most enjoyable outing to the pantomime at Norwich last Wednesday. An excited crowd

Sewing Class - 1939
from Left to Right

Barbara Lanham; Dorothy Nunn; Nancy Robinson;
Dorothy London; Olive Pooley; Pamela Barker.

Working in the School Garden - 1935

A Surviving Dinner Plate from the days when the Village Hall was owned and used as the Old Comrades' Hut - together with a Cup, Saucer and Plate set, presented by the Members of the Comrades' Association to each of the Darsham Schoolchildren at Xmas 1928.

A Silver-plated teaspoon was presented to each child at Darsham School, to comemorate the Coronation of King George VI & Queen Elizabeth.

of youngsters was transported the thirty miles by bus, this journey being made more thrilling to the children by a mechanical defect which entailed a frantic message for a new bus. In spite of this, only about five minutes of a gorgeous show were lost. The many different scenes called forth gasps of pleasure and nothing was missed by these enthralled children.

After the show, a most delightful tea was served at a nearby café, and a well contented crowd was once again on the road, arriving home soon after 7 pm.
The funds for this outing were raised by a jumble sale, whist drive and auction, all very nobly supported by the people of Darsham & district, who never fail when it is something for the children."

War was declared on Sunday 3rd September, 1939. The thoughts of the men in Whitehall had already turned to the prospect of German aggression and the possibility of war. It was feared that an attack on Britain would include the indiscriminate bombing of civilian targets. In 1937, the matter came before the Committee for Imperial Defence, whose staff projected a scenario of continuous air attack on London from the outbreak of war. They calculated that more than half a million people would be killed and double that number injured in the first two months of aerial attack. Civilian evacuation was planned.

On Friday 1st September, 1939, all teachers had been recalled early from the summer holidays. The first evacuation began, and within four days more than 1.3 million people were moved out of London alone. The first evacuees to arrive in Darsham were children from Becontree Middle School, Ilford. There were twenty boys and seven girls, plus two assistant teachers and three volunteer helpers. Another group of four boys and three girls, with their mothers and the headmaster arrived from Goodmayes School, Ilford. More mothers with children were billeted in Darsham House. Evelyn Alexander, who was by this time working at Darsham House, recalls that each of the evacuee mothers living there was given a new pram and layette by Mrs Parry-Crooke, the 'lady of the Manor House.'

Darsham School re-opened on 18th September with ninety-nine pupils and four teachers (the largest number of staff but not quite the lowest teacher/pupil ratio it had ever had). The Comrades' Hut at the other end of the Street was pressed into service, and the W.I. Hut, at the rear of the Comrades' Hut, was used as the school canteen. From 1941 it also came to be used for P.T., Games and dancing classes.

The next day the Gardening Instructor arrived at the School to

LETTER FILE - RELATING TO THE EVACUEES AT DARSHAM SCHOOL
1939 - 1940

S.R.O.Ref: 564 / 33

A copy of the answers which had been given to a questionnaire from the East Suffolk Education Committee in relation to evacuees, school numbers and organisation.

1. Becontree Middle Boys to Darsham
   2 Assistant teachers. 3 Volunteer helpers, 27 children

2. Becontree Middle Boys at Darsham
   20 boys, 7 girls

   Mrs E. Quadling, Headmistress of Darsham School No.71
   re: circulars 2/1939 & 3/1939

   2a. 20 boys & 7 girls of school age in Darsham from Becontree Middle Boys, Dagenham (Ilford Board) - Total 27
   Headmaster Mr Baldock

   Children of school age evacuated with mothers from Goodmayes School, Ilford 4 Boys & 3 Girls - Total 7
   Headmaster Mr H.W.Noble

   There are at least two other families privately evacuated of school age in the village.

   2b. No Secondary
   No Selective Central
   8 Seniors   }
   17 Juniors   }   Total 34 + 2 Private families
   9 Infants   }
   No Private School

3. A canteen for dinners for both evacuees and locals would be welcome. The W.I. Hut could be used for this. There is a separate kitchen with Valor Stove and the three helpers brought with the Ilford children are very willing to assist.

4. 17 children used to having Milk 7 paying for it.

5. There are no Free Milk children among these.

6. The Ex-servicemen who own the hut are having a meeting tonight and there is every likelihood of our being able to have this hut which is equipped with chairs, trestle tables & stove.

7. With the evacuating head (whose school is split up among Darsham Westleton, Dunwich & Middleton) I have discussed what we can try, and he is agreeable to the following being tried:

   Arrange children, both local and evacuees into two groups for morning sessions.

   All older children to be in the school building (approx 50-55 chn) and younger ones in the Mens' Hut.

   Send the under 7s home at dinner-time and divide the rest (7s - 14s) into 2 groups, taking alternate afternoons at school and in the hut, with extra help of the 2 Jnr. Teachers so that all children 7+ would be at school for normal hours.

8. I have talked with the Evacuees' headmaster, Mr Baldock, and he is in agreement with this to be tried.

9. Full agreement on this point.

10. No shortage yet (*of teachers?*) But Gladys Boreham (D.O.B.5.7.1904) living at Stone Cottage, Darsham, Supplementary has applied to teach again having taught 5 years under East Suffolk at Shotley & Trimley 13 years ago.

11. We will use separate registers *(locals and evacuees)*

****

In September 1939, 36 evacuees with adults arrived in Darsham
Permission was given to use both the W.I. Hut and the Ex-servicemens' Hut for as often and as long as they were wanted.. It was reported the W.I. Hut was to be used as a canteen for all children except those under 7s who would be sent home at dinner-time. The Hut was equipped with a three-burner stove but the services of a volunteer cook would be required.

The School was reopened on Monday 18th September in the school building and the mens' Hut.
Morning school was from 9am - 12 mid-day.

At the school were all children - both local and evacuees, aged 9+
The Head teacher, Mrs E. Quading being in charge with an
assistant teacher, Mr Daniels, *evacuees teacher*.

At the Mens' Hut were all children under 9
With teachers assistants, Miss Bone, *evacuees teacher*, and Miss E.M.Ashwell, *a Darsham teacher*.

There would be an inter-change of children between the school and the hut.
It was also suggested that any child under 7 may go home at dinner time.

The hut was to be hired to the Education Committee at a weekly rent of 5/- by Revd. Maitland (Darsham Vicar) who was the Billeting Officer for the area..

make arrangements for full-scale production, presumably all the older boys were pressed into digging.

It is difficult to obtain a general picture of the effects of evacuation on children. Various opinions are expressed to do with the removal of children from their families over long periods, a number of these concern the effects of an education away from home at boarding school. Some people thought that the less contact time there is between children and their parents, the more children will gain in self-confidence. However, there is also evidence that children's development is undermined in these circumstances. Undoubtedly some children enjoyed evacuation, but some were scarred for life by perceived hardship. One child named Joyce Phillips, who came to Darsham for a time from London in 1939 recorded her reminiscences: "Darsham School which I had to attend did not impress me very favourably. It was the first time I had seen such a small school, only two large classrooms, one for the younger ones and the other from around 9 years to 14 years. I had the year of 1939, passed my scholarship for a Girls' High School to begin in September. I was very disappointed not to be going there. This, together with the fact that my brother and I knew no other children, even the evacuees in Darsham were not from our school, coloured my attitude and left me with rather non-happy memories of both school and teacher. It was the first time ever that I was unable to get along with a teacher, it seemed to me I was always in trouble with Mrs Quadling"

From this time we get a snapshot of Mrs Quadling's attitude to collaborative work practice. In September 1939 - very soon after the arrival of those new teachers - the East Suffolk Education Committee received a complaint that Mrs Quadling was not very tactful with the London teachers and the helpers who arrived to assist with the evacuees. A Mr Claxton from the Education Committee called on Mrs Quadling and had a word with her about tact. He reported that he thought that it was probably her zeal to do the job efficiently that made her dictatorial in her methods. Perhaps she did not take kindly to outside interference in the running of 'her school'. It may have gone further than that. Mrs Quadling does not appear to have always got on well with the teachers appointed to Darsham School. One former pupil describes how she appeared to disparage a colleague several years later in 1947. Mrs Feavyour is described as being quite solemn, strict and unsmiling, but she was always kind and fair to the children . She was well respected. One might have thought that both these teachers would have been able to work well together. However, the story goes, at lunchtime and break times, the two women made their own drinks on the fires in their own classrooms and did not mix.

Meanwhile, by June 1940, the evacuees who had come from Ilford finally left Darsham. The mothers and children who had been evacuated to Darsham House also left, taking their new prams and layettes with them. Later, at the end of 1944, a second, smaller group of about a dozen evacuees came from

WESTLETON COUNCIL SCHOOL.

RE-OPENING SCHOOLS; MONDAY. 18.9.39.

1. No child to be on school premises before 8.45.a.m.

2. No child will be accepted at school who has not brought a GAS MASK.

   #### On the Way to School.
3. If an Air Raid Warning is sounded whilst a child is on the way to school, and the school is in sight or within 3 or 4 minutes running distance, the child should run to school if possible. If the child is too far from school and too far from home, he or she is to go into nearest field, lie down if any aircraft is heard passing over, and be ready to put on gas mask if any explosion is heard nearby. As soon as the All-Clear Signal is sounded child should proceed to school or home as fast as possible. Do not stay on or near main road during an Air Raid. When the Warning is given, if child is within 2 or 3 minutes distance from home, he or she should return home.

   #### Before leaving School.
4. If an Air Raid Warning is given before the end of school, the Head Teacher will retain control of all the children and not allow them away from the school premises until the All-Clear is sounded. If this means they are still on school premises when darkness falls, parents will be expected to do their best to fetch children.

   #### Lunch Hour.
5. No child staying to lunch to leave school premises without permission of Head Teacher. Parents must impress on children importance of obeying Head Teacher's instructions.

6. Afternoon Session. 1.p.m. - 3.30.p.m.

Keep carefully.

Letter sent to parents at beginning of W.W.2, a similar letter would have been sent to parents in Darsham.

Hospital Farm,
Dunwich,
Saxmundham.

The Director of Education,
Ipswich

5 Sept. '39

Dear Sir,

The Becontree Middle Boys' School Party, 12 of Ilford, Essex is stationed in four villages as follows:-

	Assistant Teachers	Voluntary Helpers	Children of All Ages	Total
Westleton	2	3	25	30
Middleton	2	3	42	47
Dunwich	1	4	36	42
Darsham	2	3	27	32
				151

Yours faithfully,
W. J. Baldock
Headmaster.

Letter from Headmaster, Becontree School to Ipswich Education Office.

London in order to escape the doodle-bug flying bombs, but in the end they did not stay for long.

A Ministry of Information leaflet of 1941 called "You can help your Country" caught the spirit of these times:

"The difference between this war and previous wars is that we are all in the front line in a struggle for the principles of freedom and justice and respect for the laws of God and honour amongst men. Whether we are in uniform or not, we are in the war. And no matter how young we are or how old we are there are jobs we can do for our country." *(Cited in Mayall & Morrow, op.cit., P.1).*

Whether children should work was debated throughout the war. Did the possible effects of a depleted education for these young children figure largely in this debate? Would their life chances be affected, and how might the economy be influenced in the long term? What could be the extent of the short-term gain for the war effort?

The war effort at Darsham achieved remarkable results. There is a note in the School Log Book that in May 1940, a Jumble Sale raised £11. 13s. 1d. for the 'Comforts Fund'. Mrs Quadling gingered the school into providing 'comforts' for sailors. These kind acts generated so much goodwill that, by way of gratitude, after the war a small minesweeper was named H.M.S. Darsham. The vessel was based in Hong

Kong, and when it was decommissioned the ship's bell was presented to the village by the Royal Navy, and is displayed in the parish church. The support of the school did not stop at comforts. 5th—10th May, 1941 was "War Weapons Week", and the school collected £635. 12s. 0d. There were annual blackberrying days and salvage collection. Amazingly, the 1941 blackberry day yielded 225½ lbs.of fruit, for which the children were paid 3d. per lb. May, 1944 brought "Salute the Soldier Week" when £274 was raised by the school.

There wasn't much in the shops that children could spend their threepences on in 1944. Sweet rationing had begun in 1940 and would continue for thirteen years, well after the end of the war. However, Mary Baillie remembers that during this time, the Rev. Maitland made himself 'very popular with the children'. She recalls that he and his housekeeper, Miss Mason, saved up their sweet ration and brought Cadbury's Chocolate to distribute among the children. Even when he retired, and he and Miss Mason moved to Ipswich, they continued this practice, returning to the village to distribute the sweets.

Darsham school was fortunate to have their wireless set. Radio broadcasts compensated for staffing difficulties. From 1940 and throughout the war, the BBC broadcast the programmes for schools entitled, "The Practice & Science of Gardening", giving detailed advice on producing food. School broadcasts also included, from September 1941, a five minutes "News Commentary." Programmes for children deliberately included children and adults talking seriously with each other. The view of children as sensible people who could 'do their bit' for the nation was reflected in a 1945 review on the work of "Children's Hour" during the war given by the radio character 'Uncle Mac' *(Derek McCulloch)*. He said it aimed:-

"To give children stability and continuity in a world of chaos and change, to give children the best music, story, drama; to encourage their war effort in savings schemes, salvage, handicraft, harvesting and safety first; to avoid too much emphasis on direct war topics or hate of enemies but focussing on the part played by men and women in the Services; to avoid creating fear, to give direct and regular religious instruction." *(Cited in Mayall & Morrow, op.cit., P.102).*

Going to the pictures provided children with more messages. David Gooderham, a pupil at Darsham School, recalls film shows in the Comrades' Hut: "A local film unit, the Holton Valley Film Company, came to the Hall once a week to show films and newsreels, most of them being out of date, but the Hall used to be full on each occasion."

David was evacuated from Ipswich to live with his grandparents, Lancelot and Alice Knights in the cottage known as 'South View' at the rear of the Fox Inn. He was entered on the Darsham School roll on 24th January, 1944 and remained until May, 1945. In his recollections *(Round by Will's Mother's Way, published in Leiston in 2000)* he recalls:

"Darsham School had two classes, the Little Room and the Big Room. The first thing that occurred was that I was instructed to write 'joined up' instead of printing, which is how I had been taught at Ipswich. The school served just the village so the pupils represented the community. Obviously there were two teachers and the Headmistress lived in the village just beyond the Smithy. Her mode of transport was a pony and trap and woe betide anyone who didn't get out of her way or who made the horse shy. The school was lit with oil lamps and heated by a coal fire in the large room and a coke-fired boiler in the small room.
There were two earth-closet toilets in small brick sheds in the playground. Gardens were located alongside and on one afternoon each week all the boys had to work in the gardens, digging, weeding, planting and cropping. Clearly, one important textbook we had was an ESEdA book dealing solely with gardening and land husbandry. As you would expect, little at the school was any different to what was found in the homes we came from. There was a water pump in the street and each morning two boys had to take a water cart to the pump, fill it and push it to the Village Hall where ladies prepared our lunches."

This extract gives us a very clear picture of the condition of the Darsham School building at the time. The physical details would be typical of many rural schools, and they would remain so until the advent of electricity, mains water, drainage and central heating. Already the provision of school meals was changing. The lunches for Darsham had in fact begun to be supplied from Yoxford from Lady Day, 1943 onwards, and there were incessant complaints for years to come about both the quantity and the quality of the food that arrived at Darsham.

The very simple provisions of the school did not affect the quality of the work drawn from its pupils by some expert teaching, involving quite novel cross-curricular lessons (as the jargon of later years would describe them). Basil Nichols, who was thirteen years old, wrote an essay in 1944. His handwriting, spelling and grammar are a credit to his teachers. The essay describes an organised bicycle ride, which was planned as an outdoor lesson. Twelve pupils, led by Mrs Quadling and Miss Beck, rode in pairs with the two teachers in front, and Jean Stammers and Mary Booth at the rear, because "they had bells on their bicycles and if anyone had trouble with their cycle, they could ring their bells to alert the teachers". Risk assessments were simple in those days. Even so, on the way home, Jean Stammers and Mary Booth must have had to ring their bells because "Olive Thurston's pedal fell off." Poor Olive Thurston!

After being shown the church ruins at Dunwich, and having tea on the cliff top, they were taken to the Coastguard Station where a Coastguard told the children about his job. He showed them a beach mine and explained how it worked, and they were also shown an aircraft spare petrol tank, which had been recovered from the beach. Two more of these spare tanks were pointed out still lying on the beach. Before returning home, the teachers led the children in games on the heath: 'Hide & Seek' and 'Come to Learn the Trade.' Basil notes that the journey home was uneventful, "except Olive Thurston's pedal fell off."

Shortly after this bicycle trip, on 12th August, 1944 Jean Brown was standing outside her home, Stone Cottage, and heard planes flying overhead, when one of the planes exploded, the force of the blast threw her backwards pinning her against a wall, while lumps of masonry fell around her. The plane had been carrying an experimental bomb, which had detonated suddenly and catastrophically. It was being piloted by Joseph Kennedy, son of the U.S. Ambassador to Gt. Britain, and brother of John F. Kennedy, future President of the United States of America.

During these years, the children experienced many of the effects of war at first hand. Darsham children saw the Army take over Darsham House, and an R.A.F. Radar Station built and operated in the parish. There were family members away from home in the Services. Everyone living near the

8th June, 1946

T0-DAY, AS WE CELEBRATE VICTORY, I send this personal message to you and all other boys and girls at school. For you have shared in the hardships and dangers of a total war and you have shared no less in the triumph of the Allied Nations.

I know you will always feel proud to belong to a country which was capable of such supreme effort; proud, too, of parents and elder brothers and sisters who by their courage, endurance and enterprise brought victory. May these qualities be yours as you grow up and join in the common effort to establish among the nations of the world unity and peace.

George R.I.

His Majesty the King's Message to Schoolchildren

I WISH TO MARK, BY THIS PERSONAL MESSAGE, my appreciation of the service you have rendered to your Country in 1939.

In the early days of the War you opened your door to strangers who were in need of shelter, & offered to share your home with them.

I know that to this unselfish task you have sacrificed much of your own comfort, & that it could not have been achieved without the loyal co-operation of all in your household. By your sympathy you have earned the gratitude of those to whom you have shown hospitality, & by your readiness to serve you have helped the State in a work of great value.

Elizabeth R

Her Majesty the Queen's Message to Householders

east coast would see damaged aircraft flying back from bombing raids, as well as German war planes and V.1. flying bombs over the parish. On the south coast there was one horrifying incident where a girls' hockey match had been machine gunned by a German fighter pilot, though mercifully without casualties. *(See H. Buckton, 'The Children's Front: The impact of the Second World War on British Children.' 2009, P.140).*

There was one more incident involving an aircraft over Darsham. In February 1945, a Flying Fortress 'Lil Edie' was flying out from Eye Airfield, laden with bombs. It caught fire over Darsham. The plane circled the village with its guns firing to warn people below. The bombs were dropped safely, causing livestock casualties only. After the crew bailed out, the plane crashed in a field opposite Darsham Garage, beyond the railway line. The children from Darsham who travelled to Sir John Leman School in Beccles every day, were on the train on their way to school, and saw it all happen. Frightened, as well as anxious, they got out at the next station and walked back home to find that thank goodness there were no casualties, only damage to windows and roofs. *(See report submitted by Pc.127, William D. Martin, Yoxford Rural Police Station, to Superintendent Hopes, Halesworth).*

'Victory in Europe' was celebrated with public holidays on 8th and 9th May, 1945, and the war with Japan ended on 15th August, following the dropping of the first Atom Bomb. Yet minor disruption to school life continued. On 8th October the school was closed for collecting Hips, and the final week of the summer holiday was postponed until November, but was designated as a week for potato picking. Perhaps this was because children wouldn't have so far to stoop?

Darsham School and Mrs Quadling had survived the war, and all sorts of memories would be taken into the future, for better or for worse. The war had come to everyone's doorstep. In total during the war, about 41,000 civilians had been killed, and 137,000 injured. Of the dead 7,736 were children. It could have been so many more. The madness of the war ended with the obliteration of Hiroshima and Nagasaki. It would be good to be able to write a grand concluding paragraph to the war years at Darsham School, but as with any school, distinction can only be revealed through the affairs of the children and their teachers. If nothing else, they had the opportunity to learn to make the best of things, and to learn to work sacrificially for the common good.

Perhaps the need to make the best of things had its effects on Mrs Quadling, effects that have caused her efforts to be recalled with severity by those who had known her. Possibly her efforts involved some considerable self-sacrifice. A book of her handwritten poems has survived, and it shows that she wrote in particular about events in life that affected her. A gentler side to her nature is shown in a poem written in 1943, mourning the death of thirteen year old Norah May Elmy.

Wreckage of B17 'Lil Edie' in field opposite Station at Darsham.

Radar Pylons at R.A.F. High Street.

R.A.F. High Street site.

Norah May was the daughter of Elvyn and Catherine Elmy of Brussels Green Farm, Darsham. Norah had been a pupil at Darsham School and had left in the summer of 1942 to continue her secondary education at Beccles.

Norah - died Nov 1943.

Dear little Norah's laid to rest,
Not far from those who loved her best,
Oh why? We cannot know yet,
There is some reason. Do not fret,
Too much. She was a lovely child,
Her ways were gentle, sweet and mild,
God called her home - too soon for us
To understand, or bear her loss.
Perhaps He needs a loyal friend,
To help him with his work that end.
There is one thing may comfort you
To know she was so staunch, so true
That all her friends from miles around,
Came here today, to Church, and found,
The sun was there to Welcome her.
The day was kind, as if to say
"We welcome you dear Norah May"
And oh! The flowers that were brought
They too were full of kindest thought.

Mrs Quadling lived in a house in the village that she had designed herself. She had some architectural training, which perhaps explains her fastidious attention to detail. It may well have been that to work in architecture had been her chosen career, which was thwarted by the Depression. Yeovil House, Mill Lane, stands as a different kind of testimony to her creative talent. This creative ability also directed towards things that she did for the pupils in her charge out of an obvious sense of caring. She made jig-saw puzzles, using magazine pictures, and is credited with making clothes for the children of a very poor family out of hand-me-downs. She is also remembered by ex-pupils as being a talented artist; one person still owns a painting; another has a sketch by Mrs Quadling in her autograph book.

From the recollections of a number of her ex-pupils, it is clear that Mrs Quadling is remembered with very mixed emotions. Some recall her kindness to them and the special attention and encouragement that they received in order to reach 'scholarship standard'. Others, although personally doing well at Darsham School, were frightened of her and of her readiness to inflict physical punishment, usually with a ruler on the back of the legs, even for such infringements as getting sums wrong. One ex-pupil recalls one poor boy, who was not the brightest in the class, being punished on an almost daily basis, often on the posterior.

In the late 1940's and early 1950's, Mrs Quadling organised the Darsham Dancing Club with Mrs Boreham, a parent, and they taught the children to dance during the winter evenings.

Mrs Quadling

Highland Dance Team
Valerie Mouser; Joy Burtenshaw; Joan Boreham
Mary Baillie

Darsham Pupils - 1952
(Teacher - Mrs Quadling)

Back Row - left to right
Eileen Robinson; Michael Mouser; Joan Boreham; Shirley Cook; Dawn Jarvis; Neil Alexander; Alan Green; John Feavyour; Tish Tovell.

Middle Row - left to right
Mary Baillie; Edward Thurston; Pat Holmes; Keith Jackson; Eve Jarvis; Rose Woolnough; Valerie Mouser.

Front Row - left to right
Peter Watling; Glenys Golding; Jill Watling; Joy Burtenshaw; Rose Hill; John Nunn.

In happier times, wartimes memories might be able to recede. Yet the children all knew that they had participated in an epic struggle, as bombs, bullets and even aeroplanes had fallen out of the sky around them. These children had played an essential part in the national effort. The greatness of this era was given eloquence in the famous words of Sir Winston Churchill, that many children in years to come would learn by heart:

> "Upon this battle depends the survival of Christian civilisation.
> Upon it depends our own British life and the long continuity of our Institutions, and our Empire.
> The whole fury and might of the enemy must very soon be turned on us.
> Hitler knows that he will have to break us in this Island, or lose the war.
> If we can stand up to him, all Europe may be freed, and the life of the world may move forward into the broad and sunlit uplands.
> But if we fail, then the whole world, including the United States, and all that we have known and cared for, will sink into the abyss of a new Dark Age made more sinister and perhaps more prolonged by the lights of perverted Science.
> Let us therefore brace ourselves to our duty,

and so bear ourselves that if the British Empire and Commonwealth last for a thousand years, men will still say,

"This was their finest hour."

Chapter Seven

Winding Down

A major political and military skill, other than that of winning an all out victory, is to deploy a rearguard action successfully whilst managing a retreat. By any standards, Mrs Quadling managed the challenge of a rearguard action well.

She had maintained educational standards during the war years, and introduced innovations in teaching methods at the school to encourage the efforts of her pupils. She had encouraged them in the war effort to provide 'comforts' for sailors - activities that had seen recognition for the village in the naming of the Royal Naval vessel H.M.S. Darsham. In spite of these things to her credit, there seemed now to be no encouragement or comfort from higher authority towards the maintenance of a thriving school community at Darsham.

A member of staff from the County Education office visited the school in 1946, and was recorded as being disgusted with the whole building and well she might have been. The residual problems of the building had never been dealt with. Indeed there had not even been a re-decoration of the interior since 1933. There had been the hope of that the difficulties with school dinners might be resolved. A new cook arrived at Yoxford school canteen where Darsham School's meals were prepared, but left within a month, and the food was as bad as ever, shortages and rationing no doubt partly to blame.

It seems that the county official could offer no help or even hope. She was asked whether anything could be done to improve the amount of light in the classrooms, which were still lit by oil lamps. Could the leaded diamond panes be replaced in order to let in more light and air? Such an improvement 'would be impossible'. Mrs Quadling also noted: "She also told me that all the teachers would HAVE to work harder. I told her that I already worked my hardest and that it would be impossible here." From the evidence of the last chapter we can believe this to be true. So every comfort would have to be fought for!

The remainder of 1946 saw changes in the post of assistant teacher until Mrs Feavyour took up the post in July, 1946. An order arrived during the summer holidays that all pupils would in future receive free milk. The fractious business of registration might be improved. Collection of milk money and dinner money took place at registration, and all discrepancies had to be noted and the account for each child kept it was often turned into a time of arduous negotiation and countermand.

The annual school blackberrying day took place on 30th September. There is no record that a dreadful winter could be predicted from the size of the harvest, but a terrible winter was about to descend. By the end of January 1947, the weather had closed in. For Mrs Quadling, at the time that she was beginning to engage in rearguard action, this might have smacked of the conditions endured during Napoleon's retreat from Moscow! Much of the term's attendance was lost, the school being closed for days at a time until the middle of March. At least a replacement water cart had at last been delivered in January so that reasonable quantities of water could be taken from the village pump near the school up to the canteen, which still remained at the Village Hall. One ex-pupil recalls that the journey had to be negotiated very carefully in order to avoid spilling too much of the water before reaching the hall.

Until now Darsham School, like so many other village schools, had been an all-age school, children of the village receiving free education until they left school at the age of fourteen. Scholarships were available for places at grammar schools, and children who gained scholarships from Darsham went to Beccles, to the Sir John Leman School. Other secondary places were available at Beccles and some children from Darsham had started to take up these places, so that the number of older children on roll was falling.

The effects of the Education Act of 1944, which re-organised secondary education throughout the country, now came into force locally. This affected numbers at Darsham School radically. From September 1947, all children over the age of eleven were to attend school in Yoxford. They would then receive free secondary education at school in Beccles. The 11 plus system was being introduced.

In September 1947, there were now only thirty-five children on the school roll. Mrs Quadling no longer had the challenge of being able to prepare children for entrance to secondary education at a higher level, or of teaching older village children who would have previously remained at Darsham School.

The loss of village schools has often been lamented. Standards of education are perhaps improved by teaching children in larger centres, and undoubtedly efficiency savings are made, but the extraordinary changes that have taken place in village communities during the past fifty years are undoubtedly due in some nature to the loss of the village school at the heart of the community. The rearguard action, which would eventually see the demise of Darsham School, would be a sad affair for Mrs Quadling to have to contemplate.

The future of the school garden was the first re-assessment that would have to be made. The older and stronger children had all gone, and with them also went the need for this particular educational tool. It was suggested that it should be grassed over for games, and flower beds would be set out. There were other more cheering events to divert the attention over the next few months. There was the Royal Wedding of

Princess Elizabeth to Prince Philip of Greece on 20th November, for which the children and staff earned a day's holiday, and there was another holiday for the children's party on 23rd January, 1948, and yet another Royal occasion on 26th April to mark the Silver Wedding of King George VI and Queen Elizabeth; this was also celebrated by a holiday for the school. In the summer holiday the school was at last distempered throughout, and the effects of fifteen years of soot and condensation were finally erased, ready for the new school year.

In September, 1948 the school roll had risen to thirty-eight, and a year later the roll increased to forty. Mrs Quadling was to have to work hard to have a few basic amenities introduced. In 1948 the school playground was re-surfaced with asphalt. In 1949, the school managers began to discuss the possibility of providing modern sanitation, though mains water would not arrive in the village until 1955, and main drainage as late as 1969 (the school records had reported cholera as late as 1923). In February, 1950 lavatory pails were replaced with Elsan chemical lavatories. They were made of sheet metal with an exhaust pipe like a chimney, vented to the outside. The toilet contained a sanitising and deodorizing solution, predominately formaldehyde (embalming fluid). Contents were disposed of in the same manner as those of the former 'bucket & chuck-it' toilets.

Electricity had arrived in the village in 1947, and in 1949 the school managers discussed the possibility of wiring the school. Sure enough, in April 1950 the school was wired and electricity was connected by the end of October.

A caretaker had been appointed to the school in 1927, among whose winter duties was the provision of wood to light the fires. The pay reflected this extra work of collecting wood, as the School Managers' Minute Book records that the caretaker was paid for six months at a winter rate, and six months at a summer rate. The winter rate was £2. 7s. 3d. per week, while in summer the rate was £1. 1s. 0d. Mrs Julia Goodchild, who lived with her husband Alfred at Lawn Cottage, Low Road, Darsham was in service as caretaker for the whole of the period between 1927 and 1950. Her retirement is recorded on 15th March 1950 in the Leiston Observer, she having served twenty-three years. She was presented with a tea service and an oak tray. Mrs Daisy Smith of Restville (now known as Daisy Cottage), The Street, Darsham now took up the post and remained as caretaker until the school was closed at the end of 1966.

In 1951, both of the school chimney stacks were repaired. Though this would obviously have been an essential piece of maintenance, the arrival of a new piano at a cost of £75 would have created more interest. It would allow further development in the curriculum through the use of song collections such as the News Chronicle Song Book. The nation's folk songs were being taught in schools following pioneering work by Ralph Vaughan Williams and Cecil Sharpe, who collected them and wrote them down before they were lost from everyday use with the coming mass-produced recorded music, and the radio.

At the end of the year, on 5th December, there was another death of a child recorded in the school register. David Burtenshaw was six years old when sadly he died of meningitis. He was the son of Robert and Olive Burtenshaw of The New Stores, The Street, Darsham.

On 15th February, 1952, the children observed a two-minute silence to mark the funeral of King George VI.

Though the new piano would encourage live performance of song and other musical activities, the old radio would be in constant demand for schools' broadcasting. During this period the BBC was broadcasting programmes that complimented the curriculum in science, history, and music as well as other subjects, and it introduced children to other cultures and customs widely different from their own horizons. It was time to replace the old wireless, and an application was made to the local Education Committee for funding. It was refused. Locally people were more generous, and through Mrs Quadling's fund raising efforts, by means of a 'Social' and private subscription, a new wireless was purchased and arrived at the beginning of 1953.

In June 1953, a three day holiday was given for the celebration of the Coronation of Queen Elizabeth II. All of the thirty-four Darsham school children took part in a decorated procession. One tableau presented 'Britannia', with two Pages, together with 'John Bull', 'Scotland', 'Ireland' and 'Wales. Another tableau portrayed 'The Red Rose of England in a Garden of Flowers'. The part of Britannia was portrayed by Joan Boreham and the Red Rose by Joy Burtenshaw. Alan Green portrayed John Bull. There were other tableaux representing 'Nursery Rhymes', 'The Land', 'Sea' and 'The Sky'. Britannia and the Red Rose unveiled the Coronation Seat in Coronation Square, The Street, Darsham, on 2nd June. (Current residents may be grateful that The Street was not permanently re-named 'Coronation Street'). The whole of the school visited Saxmundham School to see the film of the Coronation.

In July, nine children were taken to see the works then starting at the water tower at Heveningham. They watched an excavator at work on digging the trenches for the fourteen miles of pipe that would bring water to Darsham.

In that July, before the end of the school year, Darsham school won the area shield for the best improvement in savings. From the point of view of increasing prosperity of ordinary working people in the village, this represents a considerable landmark. To find that children were able to save money indicates a level of prosperity completely new in

Coronation 1953

Nursery Rhymes Float

At the Village Hall - after the Parade.

Coronation Day - 1953.

'Garden of Flowers' tableau

<u>Back row - left to right</u>
Valerie Mouser & Mary Baillie

<u>Middle Row - left to right</u>

Rosemary Woolnough; Joy Burtenshaw; Sarah Allen

<u>Front Row - left to right</u>
Monica Browning & Glenys Golding

Darsham, as until now families with children would have had very little or no spare cash for savings. One of the measures of the Welfare State introduced in 1946, was the Family Allowance, which allocated a weekly payment for children, though no payment was made for the first child. In 1952 it was raised from five shillings to eight shillings per week. Undoubtedly, such welfare payments have been hugely effective in raising living standards to levels that would have been undreamed of even a generation before. However, there were still drawbacks to the quality of provision at Darsham School.

A new fire grate was installed in the fireplace of the larger schoolroom where there were now only twenty juniors — there were ten infants in the small room. In spite of the new grate, the temperature in the large classroom could not be raised above freezing point in the New Year because the weather was so cold.

By May 1954, Mrs Quadling had served Darsham School as headmistress for twenty-one years. She had taken on the job in difficult circumstances and had guided the school through a long period of difficulties with financial restraints, poor provision, and falling rolls. She had none-the-less guided through major changes in the education of the local village children, whose educational achievements had been maintained and improved. Her rearguard action would have been completed successfully had she been able to see the school through to its closure in 1966. She died quite suddenly at home on 19th May, 1954. Her ashes were scattered in the garden of the house she had designed, Yeovil House Priory Lane, the house that she lived in throughout her tenure. The cremation at Ipswich on 22nd May had followed her funeral at Darsham Church. The funeral service had been attended by all of the Darsham school children. With her death, the story of the school was in many ways complete.

There was a period of rapid change of Headships with first a supply Headmistress, Miss M. E. Burton, who covered three months while a new appointment was advertised and made. Miss Cecily C. Piper remained in post for only seven months, and Miss F. Wright, a supply Headmistress, covered the next interregnum until the appointment of the person who was to be the last Headmistress of Darsham School, Mrs Joan Weaver, who was appointed in September, 1955. There was to be one further change of staffing when the roll fell below the level at which the school was eligible for two teacher posts. Mrs Evaline Feavyour had maintained her quiet, firm presence as infant teacher at the school, during that time, living just across the road from the school. She transferred to another post in 1960.

During this final period the school roll had fallen steadily from just below thirty pupils in 1954 to below twenty in 1960. In 1962, the roll was sixteen, in 1963, fifteen and in 1964, twelve. Twenty-one children transferred to Yoxford Primary

Coronation 1953 - 'Earth Float'

Coronation 1953 - 'Sky Float'

Children - left to right

Beatrice Woolnough; Christine Saker; Janet Childs

Driver - Mr Thurlow.

School in December 1966.

It is perhaps surprising to learn that this period was the time at which some most important facilities were finally installed, but it must be remembered that the fortune of Darsham School needs to be viewed within the general context of schools' provision during the period. East Suffolk allowed capital spending to rise, and there were 'per capita' rises so that money was available per pupil on roll to provide books and equipment. Drinking water was supplied to all schools as mains water was laid on in each locality. At Darsham, taps were installed in the porches, wall basins being fitted in 1955. The school interior was once again completely re-decorated and, for the first time, school meals were provided on site, though the washing up had to be done at the caretaker's house across the road.

In 1966, Mrs Weaver resigned as Headmistress. The school closed at the end of December, and twenty-one children were transferred to Yoxford School. All of the contents of Darsham School, except the piano, were given to Yoxford School. The land on which the school stood was found to belong to an ancient village charity, the Darsham Town Trust, so when the school was sold, this trust benefited by about £2,000 as an endowment for the future work of the charity.

Chapter Eight

And Finally . . . .

According to an article in the Suffolk Review in 1981, there was a large gathering of about four hundred gentlemen in the Parish Church at Stowmarket on 25th February, 1812. They were united in their conviction that schools should be established throughout Suffolk to promote the general education of the poor. This was the first concerted movement towards educating the children of Suffolk's manual workers. *(P. Northeast: The Provision of Elementary Education in 19th Century Rural Suffolk, in the Suffolk Review, Vol.5, No.2, 1981, pp 90 - 96).*

Darsham School came into existence in 1854 and finally closed after one hundred and twelve years, on 31st December, 1966. During these years, several generations of Darsham children were educated to, at times, a surprisingly high standard in that small, purpose built, school building.

The entries in the School Register of Admissions & Withdrawals were numbered sequentially. The last record of entry was numbered one thousand, three hundred and seven. It was dated 6th September, 1966 and related to Guy John Hopper, the son of John and Margaret Hopper of 'Nona-Me', The Street, Darsham. This last child only stayed for one term before being moved to Yoxford. At the tender age of five

Darsham Pupils - 1959
(Teachers - Mrs Weaver & Mrs Feavyour)

Back Row - left to right
Ronald Keable; Ray Freeman; Arthur Whiting; Robert Jarvis; Edward Nunn; Richard Tovell; Carol Page; Charles Pooley.

Middle Row - left to right
Carol Robinson; Margaret Watling; Ursula Brabbin; Toni Tovell; Irene Cook; Ann Baillie; Bernard Pooley; Virginia Watling.

Front Row - left to right
Julie Wright; David Watling; Christopher Cook; David Brunning; Carol Freeman; Margaret Pooley; Linda Nunn; Sonia Jarvis.

Sketch of Darsham Church by Mrs Quadling.

years, he may have had little awareness of the heritage that he briefly tasted.

Thirteen hundred children amounted to a great many individuals, even when spread out over more than a century. The authors have had the privilege of knowing ex-pupils from the 1920's through to the 1950's and even one who was born in the first decade of the 20th century. The overwhelming conclusion gained from this is that whilst it was far from perfect, mainly through lack of adequate finance, the school was a success. Children in Darsham benefited from a good general education and those who were willing and able, were coached through to a secondary education at a higher level.

Reading between the lines of this narrative, one cannot but help notice a repeating pattern of central regulation tending to suppress local initiative, as a prelude to centralisation of control followed by closure in the interests of administrative convenience. The tension between the local and the central remains part of the landscape of English life. Equally, the debate as to the nature and form and measurement of education is still ongoing.

A school is more than a place of learning; it is also a place of character formation. The children who went through Darsham School had the opportunity to learn to make the best of things and learn how to work together in and through adversity and deprivation. However, the world has changed, and one of the things for which a village school could not prepare its pupils was the anonymity of much of modern adult life. In the making of things alas, the brilliant standards of individual handicraft that could be achieved by individuals lost their significance and became undervalued in an age of mechanisation and mass-production. And concerning the individuality of character, it has been said of so many old villagers that they were 'characters'. It would have been their schooling (not their educational qualifications) that gave them the initial confidence to become 'characters'.

Darsham School was a special place. Above all, the conclusion is overwhelming that, despite the strict discipline enforced in former days, it was a happy school. Those pupils who have reservations about certain disciplinary practices and those enforcing that discipline, still say that they enjoyed their school days and as is shown in these pages, their school days are still fresh in their memories.

We have one opinion of the school and its pupils from a teacher, the controversial Mrs Quadling, respected and feared in equal measure by her pupils. A poem that she wrote in her private poetry book in May, 1946 shows her affection for the school and for her pupils. So then it is fitting that this poem should, for the first time, be published in this volume as a tribute to all of those who taught and were taught, in **"Our Village School"**.

The Village School

"What a quaint building!" you hear folk say
As they wander along just enjoying the day.
But do come inside and see what goes on
You may be in time to join in a song.

Two rooms! Is that all?" Yes indeed but too true,
With kiddies from four to fourteen in too.
"But how ever do you manage to teach all those ages?"
You just do your best; you put them in stages.

There's Johnnie who can't tell an 'it' from an 'at',
And Tommy, you never quite know what he's at.
There's Ann, who just sits and plays with the beads,
And Harry & Phyllis with all sorts of needs.

There's Peggy, who's ready for fractions now,
Besides lazy Ron who still can't spell "cow".
There are some doing hygiene, some drawing maps,
Some knitting, some singing, some sewing on snaps.

Yes, sure it is quaint, with that I'll agree,
But for all that it's just a grand family
of kids of all ages, all headed together

To learn all they can and to find out how to weather,
The storms and the troubles that sure will befall them
When they leave school at fourteen,
 their future before them."

A Postscript to our Darsham Village Trilogy

Never before has there been such a widespread awareness of the size and age of the universe. So it may seem strange that our three books have focussed on the struggles and achievements of our tiny village during the second millennium. But it is from where we stand that we are challenged to make sense of our existence and of the universe.

Our three titles derive from a verse in the hymn 'O God, our help in ages past.' The verse (with our three titles underlined) runs:

> "A thousand ages in thy sight
> are **like an evening gone,**
> Short as **the watch that ends the night
> before the rising sun.**"

The rising sun can be an emblem for us of all the hope that we should rightly hold for the future.

Education, the subject of this third book, has changed our lives and our expectations. We are now better equipped than ever to live creatively and with wisdom. But it is up to us to capitalise on our education by using our knowledge and our abilities in the service of God and of humankind. At the dawn of the second millennium in the year 1001, the struggles for survival in our parish were interwoven with fear and uncertainty.

At the start of the third millennium, we know that Darsham may never loom large on the world stage. However, our three books have given a clear picture of the roots of our community, so that we can be better placed to invest our energy and enthusiasm in the Darsham of the future.